CW01083439

Quit Wasting Cash: Smart Habits for Better Spending

Roseanne Godkin

Published by Roseanne Godkin, 2024.

QUIT WASTING CASH: SMART HABITS FOR BETTER SPENDING

First edition. October 1, 2024.

Copyright © 2024 Roseanne Godkin.

ISBN: 979-8227589835

Written by Roseanne Godkin.

Also by Roseanne Godkin

Quit Wasting Cash: Smart Habits for Better Spending

Chapter 1: Understanding Conscious Consumerism

Defining Conscious Consumerism

Conscious consumerism is a philosophy that encourages individuals to make informed decisions about their purchases, emphasizing the impact of their choices on society and the environment. This approach goes beyond merely seeking the lowest price; it involves a deeper consideration of how products are made, who makes them, and the broader consequences of consumption patterns. By engaging in conscious consumerism, individuals can align their spending habits with their values, promoting sustainability, ethical practices, and social responsibility.

At its core, conscious consumerism is about awareness. It encourages consumers to educate themselves about the brands they support and the products they buy. This means understanding the supply chain, labor practices, and environmental policies of companies. By choosing to support businesses that prioritize ethical sourcing, fair labor practices, and sustainable production methods, consumers can play a pivotal role in shaping market trends. This shift in mindset not only benefits the individual but also fosters a culture of accountability among businesses, pushing them toward more responsible practices.

Minimalist living and decluttering are closely tied to the principles of conscious consumerism. By adopting a minimalist approach, individuals can focus on quality over quantity, prioritizing items that serve a purpose or bring joy. This mindset encourages consumers to be selective about their purchases, reducing clutter and waste in their lives. When individuals embrace the idea that less is more, they often find themselves making more meaningful purchases that reflect their true needs and values, rather than succumbing to impulse buys or societal pressures.

Mindful consumerism also intersects with budgeting techniques, as it requires individuals to assess their spending habits critically. By setting a budget that reflects their values, consumers can allocate funds toward ethical and sustainable products while minimizing expenditures on unnecessary or harmful items. This conscious approach to budgeting not only helps individuals save money but also empowers them to make choices that resonate with their personal beliefs and lifestyle goals.

In the context of today's consumer landscape, understanding conscious consumerism is essential for navigating various spending options, from subscription services to DIY solutions. By being intentional about where and how they spend their money, consumers can support eco-friendly alternatives, thrift and resell items, and reduce impulse purchases. Ultimately, conscious consumerism fosters a sense of empowerment, enabling individuals to take control of their spending habits and contribute to a more sustainable and equitable world.

The Impact of Consumer Choices

Consumer choices wield significant power in shaping not only personal finances but also the broader economic landscape. Every purchase made reflects individual values, priorities, and the willingness to support specific practices or industries. When consumers decide to buy products that are sustainably sourced, ethically produced, or budget-friendly, they send a clear message to companies about the types of practices they endorse. This collective behavior can lead to a shift in market trends, prompting businesses to adopt more responsible practices in order to meet consumer demand.

Mindful consumerism plays a pivotal role in reducing unnecessary spending. By being conscious of what we buy, we can differentiate between needs and wants. This distinction is crucial in avoiding impulse purchases, which often lead to buyer's remorse and financial strain. Adopting a more intentional approach to shopping encourages individuals to evaluate each purchase critically, leading to more fulfilling and financially sound decisions. The impact of this mindset extends beyond personal budgets; it fosters a culture where companies are encouraged to provide quality over quantity.

Minimalist living and decluttering advocate for a lifestyle where less truly can be more. By consciously choosing to limit possessions, consumers can reduce spending and focus on what genuinely adds value to their lives. This shift not only lightens physical spaces but also alleviates mental clutter, allowing for a more peaceful existence. In this context, consumer choice becomes a tool for empowerment, enabling individuals to reclaim time and resources that can be redirected toward experiences, relationships, and personal growth rather than material accumulation.

Sustainable and eco-friendly alternatives are gaining traction as consumers become more aware of their environmental impact. Choices made at the point of sale can contribute to a larger movement towards sustainability, encouraging companies to prioritize eco-conscious practices. Whether opting for reusable products, local produce, or brands that emphasize ethical sourcing, consumers can play a significant role in driving demand for greener options. This shift not only benefits the environment but can also lead to long-term savings, as sustainable products often focus on durability and longevity.

Lastly, reselling, thrifting, and budgeting techniques can transform the way consumers approach spending. By embracing second-hand options and prioritizing thoughtful purchases, individuals can save money while also reducing waste. Strategies such as meal planning and careful navigation of subscription services further enhance this frugal mindset, allowing consumers to maximize their resources. The cumulative effect of these choices fosters a community of informed spenders who prioritize value and sustainability, ultimately leading to a more responsible and financially secure society.

Benefits of Mindful Purchasing

Mindful purchasing is the practice of making conscious decisions about what to buy, focusing on necessity, value, and sustainability. One of the primary benefits of this approach is the significant reduction in impulse spending. By taking the time to evaluate the need for an item before making a purchase, individuals can avoid the common traps set by marketing strategies that encourage hasty decisions. This shift in mindset cultivates a more intentional relationship with money, ultimately leading to better financial health.

Another important benefit of mindful purchasing is the enhancement of personal values through consumer choices. When individuals prioritize buying from ethical brands or choosing sustainable products, they reinforce their commitment to social and environmental responsibility. This alignment between purchases and personal values fosters a sense of fulfillment that transcends mere ownership of goods. As consumers become more aware of their impact, they are empowered to support businesses that prioritize ethical practices, contributing to a more sustainable economy.

Additionally, mindful purchasing encourages a minimalist lifestyle, which can lead to a more organized and less cluttered living space. By carefully curating possessions and making thoughtful purchases, individuals can create an environment that reflects their true needs and desires. This process of decluttering not only alleviates stress but also enhances the overall quality of life. A minimalist approach helps individuals appreciate what they have rather than constantly seeking more, promoting contentment and reducing the cycle of consumerism.

Budgeting techniques can also be significantly improved through mindful purchasing. By implementing strategies such as creating a shopping list, setting a budget for discretionary spending, and evaluating potential purchases against established financial goals, consumers can allocate their resources more effectively. This foresight enables individuals to make informed decisions that align with their financial objectives, ultimately leading to better management of everyday expenses. As a result, mindful purchasing becomes a powerful tool in achieving long-term financial stability.

Lastly, mindful purchasing can enhance the experience of DIY solutions and thrifting. When individuals approach shopping with a mindful attitude, they are more likely to seek out unique, second-hand items that serve a purpose or can be transformed into something new. This not only fosters creativity but also supports sustainable practices by reducing waste. Embracing a mindful approach to purchasing allows consumers to enjoy the thrill of finding hidden gems while promoting a circular economy, where items are reused, repurposed, and valued for their potential rather than discarded.

Chapter 2: Stop Spending Money on Stupid Shit

Identifying Emotional Triggers

Identifying emotional triggers is a crucial step in mastering your spending habits and avoiding unnecessary expenses. Often, the decisions we make about money are not purely financial; they are deeply intertwined with our emotions. Recognizing what prompts you to spend can illuminate patterns that lead to impulsive purchases. For many, feelings of stress, boredom, or even happiness can trigger a desire to buy something as a means of coping or celebrating. By pinpointing these emotional drivers, you can take proactive steps to mitigate their influence on your financial decisions.

One effective method for identifying your emotional triggers is to maintain a spending journal. In this journal, you can record each purchase along with the emotions you were experiencing at the time. Over a few weeks, patterns will likely emerge, revealing specific emotional states that lead to spending. For instance, if you notice that you frequently shop online during moments of anxiety or loneliness, this insight can help you identify healthier alternatives for coping, such as exercising or engaging in a hobby. This practice encourages mindfulness and allows you to recognize the difference between a want and a need.

Mindful consumerism involves being aware of your emotional state before making a purchase. Before you buy, pause and ask yourself why you feel compelled to spend. Are you trying to fill a void or reward yourself for a tough day? By reframing your perspective, you can begin to prioritize your emotional well-being over momentary gratification. This not only helps prevent impulse buys but also fosters a more intentional approach to shopping, aligning your purchases with your values and long-term goals.

In addition to self-reflection, seeking support from friends or family can enhance your understanding of emotional triggers. Conversations about spending habits often reveal shared experiences and insights. Engaging in discussions about budgeting techniques or minimalist living can provide different perspectives on how to approach your finances. Such support systems can hold you accountable and encourage you to think twice before succumbing to emotional spending. Surrounding yourself with individuals who prioritize mindful consumerism can also inspire you to adopt similar habits.

Lastly, consider incorporating strategies for reducing impulse purchases into your daily routine. Techniques such as creating a shopping list before heading to the store, implementing a waiting period for non-essential items, or even setting a specific budget for discretionary spending can help you manage emotional triggers effectively. By taking these steps, you empower yourself to make informed decisions rather than reacting emotionally. This shift not only aids in decluttering your finances but also contributes to a more sustainable and fulfilling lifestyle, ultimately aligning with your goals of ethical shopping and mindful consumption.

Recognizing Marketing Manipulation

Recognizing marketing manipulation requires a keen awareness of the tactics employed by advertisers to influence consumer behavior. Many people fall prey to these strategies without realizing it, often leading to unnecessary spending on products that do not enhance their lives. Marketing manipulation can take various forms, from persuasive language and imagery to limited-time offers that create a false sense of urgency. Understanding these techniques is the first step towards making informed purchasing decisions, ultimately aligning with the principles of mindful consumerism and frugal living.

One common tactic used in marketing is the appeal to emotions. Advertisers often craft narratives that evoke feelings of happiness, nostalgia, or even fear. For instance, a brand may present its product as essential for achieving a particular lifestyle or happiness, making consumers feel inadequate without it. By recognizing these emotional triggers, individuals can take a step back and evaluate whether they genuinely need the product or if they are being swayed by an emotional appeal. This awareness can significantly reduce the likelihood of impulse purchases and encourage more intentional spending practices.

Another prevalent strategy is the use of scarcity and urgency. Marketers often create a false sense of scarcity by suggesting that a product is in limited supply or available for a short time only. Phrases like "limited edition" or "only a few left in stock" can prompt consumers to act quickly, often leading to hasty decisions that do not align with their budgetary goals. Being aware of this manipulation can empower consumers to resist the urge to buy on impulse and instead take the time to research and reflect on their spending choices.

Social proof is another powerful influence in marketing that can lead to misguided purchases. When consumers see that a product is popular or has received positive reviews from others, they may feel pressured to conform and make a purchase. However, it is crucial to recognize that popularity does not equate to necessity or quality. Evaluating products based on personal needs, rather than the opinions of others, can help individuals focus on what truly adds value to their lives, aligning with minimalist living and sustainable practices.

Lastly, understanding the role of branding and packaging can help consumers see through marketing manipulation. Companies invest heavily in creating appealing packaging and strong brand identities that can sway purchasing decisions. Recognizing that these elements are designed to attract attention rather than indicate quality can help consumers make more rational choices. By prioritizing functionality and sustainability over flashy branding, individuals can embrace a more mindful approach to shopping, ultimately leading to better spending habits and a more intentional lifestyle.

Strategies for Cutting Out Impulse Buys

Identifying the triggers that lead to impulse buying is a crucial first step in cutting out unnecessary expenditures. These triggers can range from emotional responses, such as stress or boredom, to environmental cues, like attractive displays in stores or targeted advertisements online. By becoming aware of these influences, you can develop strategies to counteract them. Keeping a journal to track when and why you make impulse purchases can help identify patterns and enable you to address the root causes of your spending. This awareness empowers you to create a more mindful approach to shopping, allowing you to differentiate between genuine needs and fleeting desires.

Implementing a shopping list is an effective way to combat impulse buys. Before heading to the store or browsing online, take the time to compile a list of necessary items based on your actual needs and budget. Stick to this list strictly, and avoid any detours into areas that could tempt you to spend on non-essential items. This practice not only helps in maintaining focus but also instills discipline in your spending habits. Putting your list in a visible place, whether physically or digitally, can serve as a constant reminder of your goals and priorities, reducing the likelihood of straying into impulse purchases.

Another strategy is to establish a waiting period before making any non-essential purchases. This period can range from 24 hours to a week, allowing time to reflect on whether the item is truly needed or just a fleeting desire. During this waiting period, consider alternatives such as borrowing the item, renting it, or even waiting for a sale. This approach not only helps in curbing impulse spending but also encourages a more thoughtful consideration of purchases, fostering a mindset of mindful consumerism. By delaying gratification, you may find that the initial urge to buy dissipates, leading to more conscious spending decisions.

Creating a budget that accounts for discretionary spending is essential for anyone looking to minimize impulse purchases. Allocate a specific amount of money each month for non-essential items, allowing yourself the freedom to spend within those limits without guilt. Knowing you have a designated budget can help you feel more in control of your finances and reduce the anxiety that often leads to impulse buying. Additionally, tracking your spending against this budget helps reinforce positive habits and highlights areas where adjustments may be needed, ultimately supporting your goal of smarter spending.

Lastly, consider embracing a minimalist lifestyle as a way to reduce the temptation to buy impulsively. By simplifying your living space and focusing on quality over quantity, you can cultivate an environment that discourages unnecessary purchases. Surrounding yourself with fewer possessions can help you appreciate what you already own, making it easier to resist the allure of new items. This shift in mindset encourages a sustainable approach to consumerism, reinforcing the value of ethical shopping and thoughtful spending choices that align with your overall financial goals.

Chapter 3: Embracing Minimalist Living and Decluttering

The Philosophy of Minimalism

The philosophy of minimalism centers on the idea of simplifying one's life by reducing possessions, distractions, and commitments to the essentials. At its core, minimalism advocates for a lifestyle that prioritizes quality over quantity. This is particularly relevant in an era where consumer culture often encourages excessive spending on items that lack true value. Embracing minimalism allows individuals to focus on what truly matters to them, fostering a sense of clarity and purpose that can lead to more intentional spending habits.

In the context of budgeting techniques for everyday expenses, minimalism serves as a powerful framework. By identifying and eliminating unnecessary expenditures, individuals can allocate their financial resources more effectively. This shift not only involves cutting back on impulse buys but also encourages a thoughtful approach to essential purchases. When one adopts a minimalist mindset, every transaction becomes a deliberate choice, reinforcing the importance of each dollar spent and its alignment with personal values and goals.

Minimalist living also intersects with the principles of mindful consumerism and ethical shopping. When individuals commit to purchasing only what they need, they become more aware of the impact their choices have on the environment and society. This awareness can lead to a preference for sustainable and eco-friendly alternatives, as well as support for local businesses that prioritize ethical practices. By choosing quality products that last longer and serve a purpose, minimalists not only reduce waste but also contribute to a more sustainable economy.

Decluttering is another essential aspect of minimalism that resonates with the desire to stop spending money on unnecessary items.

A cluttered space often leads to a cluttered mind, making it difficult to focus on what is truly important. By systematically decluttering, individuals can create a more serene environment that promotes mindfulness and intentional living. This process can also reveal items that can be resold or donated, further contributing to a cycle of .sustainability and reducing the urge to make new purchases Finally, the philosophy of minimalism supports strategies for reducing impulse purchases, a common pitfall for many consumers. By cultivating a mindset that values experiences over possessions, individuals can learn to pause and assess their motivations before making a purchase. Techniques such as creating a waiting period for non-essential items, practicing gratitude for what one already owns, and engaging in frugal meal planning can help reinforce this philosophy. Ultimately, minimalism empowers individuals to reclaim their time, money, and energy, leading to a more fulfilling and .financially savvy lifestyle

Steps to Declutter Your Space

To effectively declutter your space, the first step is to establish clear goals. Identify the areas in your home that require attention and determine what you hope to achieve through decluttering. This might involve creating a more organized environment, reducing the amount of stuff you own, or making space for new items that serve a purpose. By having specific objectives, you can maintain focus and motivation throughout the process. Write down your goals to have a visual reminder of what you are working towards, which can be a powerful .tool for keeping you on track

Next, implement a systematic approach to decluttering. Begin with one area at a time—this could be a room, a specific closet, or even a single drawer. Tackle smaller spaces first to build momentum and confidence. As you sort through your items, categorize them into three groups: keep, donate, or discard. Be honest with yourself about what you truly need and use. If an item hasn't been touched in the past year, it's likely not serving a purpose in your life. By breaking the process into manageable tasks, you can avoid feeling overwhelmed and make steady .progress

Once you have sorted your items, it's time to deal with the "donate" and "discard" piles. Research local charities and organizations that accept donations, and schedule a drop-off or pick-up if possible. This not only helps your community but also reinforces your commitment to reducing clutter. For items that are broken or no longer usable, consider environmentally friendly disposal methods. Many areas have recycling programs that accept various materials, ensuring that your discarded items don't end up in a landfill. Taking these steps contributes to a more sustainable lifestyle while helping you clear your .space

After decluttering, focus on maintaining your newly organized environment. Establish a one-in-one-out rule to prevent future clutter from accumulating. This means that for every new item you bring into your home, you must remove an existing one. Additionally, regularly schedule decluttering sessions—perhaps monthly or quarterly—to reassess your belongings and ensure that you remain aligned with your minimalist goals. This proactive approach not only keeps your space tidy but also helps cultivate mindful consumer habits, making you .more selective about what you choose to purchase

Lastly, embrace the benefits of your decluttered space by creating a home that reflects your values and lifestyle. Consider how each item in your space contributes to your well-being and aligns with your goals of mindful consumerism. This may involve investing in sustainable and eco-friendly alternatives that enhance your living environment while reducing waste. By surrounding yourself with meaningful possessions and practicing intentional spending, you can enjoy a more fulfilling and organized life, ultimately leading to better financial habits and a .greater sense of peace in your home

Benefits of a Minimalist Lifestyle

A minimalist lifestyle offers a multitude of benefits that extend beyond mere aesthetics or personal preference; it fundamentally transforms how individuals interact with their belongings and finances. By embracing minimalism, one can significantly reduce clutter, leading to a more organized and peaceful living environment. This newfound clarity can enhance focus and productivity, allowing individuals to devote their time and energy to pursuits that genuinely matter to them, rather than being bogged down by the distractions of excess possessions.

Financially, minimalism encourages smarter spending habits. By prioritizing quality over quantity, individuals learn to invest in items that truly serve a purpose and bring joy, rather than succumbing to the allure of trendy but unnecessary purchases. This shift in perspective not only decreases overall expenditure but also fosters a sense of financial freedom. With fewer possessions, individuals often find it easier to manage their budgets and allocate funds towards experiences, savings, or sustainable investments, rather than accumulating material goods that offer fleeting satisfaction.

Moreover, adopting a minimalist approach can lead to a more mindful consumerism. As individuals become more aware of their purchasing habits, they can make intentional choices that align with their values. This means opting for ethical shopping practices, supporting sustainable brands, and choosing eco-friendly alternatives. Such decisions not only benefit the individual but also contribute to a larger movement towards responsible consumption, promoting a healthier planet and community.

The benefits of minimalism extend to practical aspects of daily life, particularly in areas such as meal planning and cooking. By streamlining kitchen tools and ingredients, home cooks can simplify their meal preparation process, leading to healthier eating habits and reduced food waste. Minimalist meal planning encourages creativity and resourcefulness, allowing individuals to make the most of what they have rather than relying on convenience foods or takeout, which can lead to unnecessary spending.

Finally, minimalism can be a powerful antidote to impulse purchases and the overwhelming nature of modern consumer culture. By cultivating a mindset of intentionality, individuals can develop strategies for resisting the temptation to buy on a whim. This can involve setting clear priorities, understanding the difference between needs and wants, and finding alternative ways to satisfy the desire for novelty or excitement. By fostering a minimalist lifestyle, individuals not only enhance their financial well-being but also contribute to a more sustainable and meaningful way of living.

Chapter 4: Budgeting Techniques for Everyday Expenses

Creating a Personal Budget

Creating a personal budget is an essential step toward regaining control over your finances and aligning your spending habits with your values and goals. A well-structured budget serves as a roadmap, guiding you through your monthly expenses while helping you identify areas where you can cut back on unnecessary expenditures. To begin the budgeting process, start by gathering all financial information, including income sources, fixed expenses such as rent or mortgage payments, and variable costs like groceries and entertainment. This comprehensive view of your finances will provide a solid foundation for creating a realistic budget that reflects your lifestyle and priorities.

Once you have collected your financial data, categorize your expenses into essential and non-essential items. Essential expenses include necessities like housing, utilities, groceries, transportation, and insurance, while non-essential expenses encompass discretionary spending on dining out, entertainment, and shopping. This classification helps you see which areas of your budget are flexible. Emphasizing the importance of mindful consumerism, focus on reducing spending in non-essential categories. This approach aligns with minimalist living principles, encouraging you to prioritize experiences and meaningful purchases over material possessions.

Next, set clear financial goals that guide your budgeting decisions. These goals can range from saving for a vacation, building an emergency fund, or investing in sustainable products and services. By establishing specific, measurable, achievable, relevant, and time-bound (SMART) goals, you create a motivating framework that can help curb impulse purchases and encourage more thoughtful spending habits. Incorporating ethical shopping practices into your budget can also enhance your sense of fulfillment, as you invest in products and services that align with your values.

With your budget in place, monitor your spending regularly to ensure you stay on track. This practice not only reinforces your commitment to your financial goals but also helps identify any potential areas for adjustment. Utilize budgeting apps or spreadsheets to track your expenses, making it easier to visualize your financial situation. Additionally, consider implementing DIY solutions for home and lifestyle projects, as these can save money while promoting sustainability. By embracing frugal meal planning and cooking, you can further reduce grocery costs, allowing you to allocate more funds toward your financial goals.

Lastly, review and adjust your budget periodically to reflect any changes in your financial circumstances or goals. Life is dynamic, and your budget should adapt accordingly. This flexibility allows you to navigate subscription services wisely, ensuring you're only paying for what adds value to your life. By continuously refining your budget, you enhance your financial literacy and cultivate habits that support a more intentional and fulfilling lifestyle. Ultimately, creating a personal budget empowers you to quit wasting cash and make more informed choices about your spending.

Tracking Your Spending

Tracking your spending is a fundamental step toward achieving financial clarity and control. It involves meticulously recording every expense, no matter how small, to understand where your money goes each month. By doing this, you can identify unnecessary expenditures or patterns that may be draining your finances. Whether you're looking to stop spending money on frivolous items or seeking to adopt a minimalist lifestyle, having a clear picture of your expenses can help you make informed decisions about your spending habits.

To effectively track your spending, start by choosing a method that suits your lifestyle. You can use traditional pen and paper, a spreadsheet, or digital budgeting apps that automatically categorize your expenses. The goal is to find a system that you will consistently use. Many apps even provide insights into your spending habits, making it easier to spot areas for improvement. No matter the method, consistency is key. Set aside time weekly to review your transactions and ensure that they align with your financial goals.

Once you have a tracking system in place, categorize your expenses to gain better insight into your spending patterns. Categories can include essentials like groceries and utilities, as well as discretionary spending on dining out or entertainment. This categorization allows you to see at a glance where you might be overspending and where you can cut back. For those interested in mindful consumerism, recognizing which categories are aligned with your values can help reinforce better spending choices, pushing you toward more ethical and sustainable purchases.

Implementing a budget based on your tracked spending can further enhance your financial health. A budget serves as a guideline that helps you allocate your funds thoughtfully, ensuring that you prioritize essential expenses while limiting discretionary spending. This is particularly useful for those looking to reduce impulse purchases or navigate subscription services wisely. By establishing clear limits, you can enjoy your life without the anxiety of overspending or accruing debt.

Lastly, regularly reviewing your spending can help reinforce your commitment to better financial habits. Set monthly check-ins to evaluate your progress, making adjustments to your budget as necessary. This practice not only keeps you accountable but also allows you to celebrate small victories along the way. By tracking your spending diligently, you can cultivate a more mindful approach to your finances, leading to a healthier, more sustainable lifestyle that aligns with your values and goals.

Tips for Sticking to Your Budget

To successfully stick to your budget, the first step is to create a realistic and detailed budget that reflects your true income and expenses. Begin by tracking all your spending for at least a month to identify patterns and areas where you may be overspending. Categorize your expenses into fixed costs, such as rent and utilities, and variable costs, such as groceries and entertainment. This will provide clarity on where your money is going and help you allocate funds more effectively. Adjust your budget as necessary to align it with your financial goals, ensuring it is neither too strict nor overly lenient.

A key strategy for maintaining your budget is to set specific financial goals. Whether you aim to save for a vacation, pay off debt, or build an emergency fund, having clear objectives will motivate you to adhere to your budget. Break larger goals into smaller, achievable milestones to enhance your sense of accomplishment. As you reach these milestones, celebrate your progress, which can further reinforce your commitment to your financial plan. Remember, the more meaningful your goals, the more likely you are to stay focused and disciplined in your spending habits.

Incorporating mindful consumerism into your daily life can significantly aid in sticking to your budget. Before making a purchase, ask yourself if the item is truly necessary or if it's simply an impulse buy. Develop a habit of waiting at least 24 hours before committing to non-essential purchases. This cooling-off period allows you to evaluate whether the item aligns with your financial goals and lifestyle. Additionally, consider adopting a minimalist mindset by focusing on quality over quantity. Invest in fewer, high-quality items that enhance your life, rather than accumulating possessions that contribute to clutter and financial strain.

Utilizing DIY solutions can also support your budgeting efforts. Many household items can be made or repaired at home, saving you money and reducing waste. From homemade cleaning products to upcycled furniture, embracing DIY projects not only fosters creativity but also reinforces a sustainable lifestyle. Explore online resources and community workshops to learn new skills that can help you tackle home improvement projects or create gifts and decor. This approach not only saves money but also allows you to enjoy the satisfaction of creating something with your own hands.

Finally, regularly review and adjust your budget to ensure it remains relevant to your changing circumstances. Life events, such as a new job, a move, or a shift in family dynamics, can impact your financial situation, making it essential to stay flexible. Schedule monthly check-ins to analyze your spending, assess your progress toward financial goals, and make necessary adjustments. By maintaining an open dialogue with your budget, you cultivate a proactive approach to your finances that encourages accountability and fosters long-term financial health.

Chapter 5: DIY Solutions for Home and Lifestyle

Cost-Effective DIY Projects

Cost-effective DIY projects offer a practical solution for those looking to save money while enhancing their living spaces and lifestyles. Many people often feel the pressure to spend on overpriced home decor, furniture, and other necessities that can easily be created or improved through simple, budget-friendly DIY endeavors. By taking the time to research and implement these projects, individuals can not only cut costs but also embrace a more minimalist lifestyle that emphasizes functionality and personal touch over consumerism.

One of the most straightforward DIY projects involves repurposing items that may otherwise be discarded. For instance, old wooden pallets can be transformed into stylish furniture pieces, such as coffee tables or garden benches. Similarly, glass jars can be converted into beautiful storage solutions for the kitchen or bathroom. These projects not only reduce waste but also promote sustainable living by encouraging the use of materials that are already available. By tapping into creativity and resourcefulness, individuals can create unique items that reflect their personal style without the accompanying financial strain.

Another area where DIY projects shine is in home improvement. Simple tasks such as painting a room, creating an accent wall with removable wallpaper, or updating hardware on cabinets can drastically change the feel of a space without the need for professional help. These projects often require minimal investment in materials and tools, yet they yield significant results. Additionally, engaging in home improvement not only boosts the aesthetic appeal but also increases the overall value of the property, making it a wise investment for the future.

DIY solutions extend beyond physical projects; they can also encompass skills such as sewing or crafting. Learning to mend clothes or create new garments can save a substantial amount of money that would otherwise be spent on fast fashion. By acquiring these skills, consumers can cultivate a sustainable wardrobe that minimizes waste and promotes ethical shopping habits. Furthermore, homemade gifts crafted from the heart, such as knitted scarves or personalized photo albums, can replace expensive store-bought items, reinforcing the idea that meaningful gestures do not have to come with a hefty price tag. Finally, embracing cost-effective DIY projects encourages mindfulness in consumer habits. By focusing on creating and repurposing, individuals become more aware of their purchasing decisions and the impact of mindless spending. This shift in mindset can lead to a more intentional approach to shopping, steering clear of impulse purchases and promoting a lifestyle centered around thoughtful consumption. As a result, not only does one save money, but they also cultivate a sense of satisfaction and fulfillment from the items they choose to keep and create.

Upcycling and Repurposing Ideas

Upcycling and repurposing have gained traction as practical solutions for reducing waste while saving money. Every day, countless items end up in landfills, contributing to environmental degradation and unnecessary spending. By creatively transforming these items, individuals can not only declutter their homes but also find innovative ways to utilize what they already own. This approach aligns perfectly with the principles of minimalism and mindful consumerism, allowing you to embrace a lifestyle that values creativity over consumption. One of the simplest ways to start upcycling is by reimagining furniture. Instead of purchasing new pieces, consider refurbishing old ones. A coat of paint can breathe new life into a tired chair or table, while adding new hardware can modernize a dresser. Pallets, often discarded, can be transformed into stylish shelves or outdoor seating. These projects not only enhance your living space but also provide a sense of accomplishment and personal touch that new items often lack.

Textiles also offer numerous upcycling opportunities. Old curtains can be converted into cushion covers, while worn-out jeans can be turned into trendy bags or quilts. By utilizing fabric scraps, you can create unique home décor items without the need for new materials. This practice reduces waste and encourages creativity, fostering a mindset that values resourcefulness over mindless purchasing. Additionally, engaging in textile upcycling can lead to significant savings on home goods and gifts.

In the kitchen, repurposing can be particularly rewarding. Glass jars from sauces or jams can be used for storage, while leftover food can be creatively transformed into new meals. For instance, vegetable scraps can become nutritious broths, and stale bread can be turned into croutons. These practices not only minimize food waste but also enable effective meal planning, aligning with frugal cooking strategies. By viewing food through the lens of upcycling, you can reduce grocery bills while enjoying diverse and inventive meals.

Finally, embracing upcycling and repurposing can cultivate a community-oriented mindset. Organizing swap meets or participating in local crafting groups can help share ideas and resources. Websites and social media platforms offer countless inspiration and tutorials, making it easier to learn and share your creations. By engaging with others in this way, you can foster connections while promoting sustainable practices. This communal aspect not only enriches your life but also supports a shift towards more mindful consumption patterns that benefit both individuals and the planet.

Benefits of DIY Living

DIY living offers numerous benefits that extend far beyond the immediate satisfaction of creating something with your own hands.

One of the most significant advantages is the substantial financial savings that can be achieved by opting for do-it-yourself solutions. Many everyday items and services, from home repairs to personal care products, can be made or fixed at a fraction of the cost of store-bought alternatives. By embracing DIY projects, individuals can significantly reduce their expenditure, allowing them to allocate their finances toward more meaningful experiences or investments.

In addition to financial benefits, DIY living promotes a sense of accomplishment and self-sufficiency. Completing a project, whether it's building a piece of furniture or crafting a gift, instills a sense of pride that is often lacking in consumer-driven lifestyles. This empowerment can lead to increased confidence in one's abilities, encouraging individuals to tackle more complex tasks and projects over time. As people develop new skills, they not only enhance their capabilities but also cultivate a mindset of resourcefulness that is invaluable in today's fast-paced world.

Moreover, DIY living aligns closely with the principles of minimalism and decluttering. Engaging in do-it-yourself projects often necessitates a thorough examination of what one truly needs versus what is simply accumulated clutter. This process encourages a more intentional approach to consumption, fostering a lifestyle where individuals prioritize quality over quantity. As they create or repurpose items, they learn to appreciate the value of simplicity and the benefits of having fewer possessions, ultimately leading to a more organized and serene living environment.

Sustainable and eco-friendly practices are also a cornerstone of DIY living. By making items from scratch or upcycling existing materials, individuals contribute to reducing waste and minimizing their environmental footprint. Many DIY projects can incorporate recycled or natural materials, aligning with the growing interest in mindful consumerism. This conscious choice to create rather than

consume fosters a deeper connection with the materials used and a
greater appreciation for the resources that go into everyday products.
Lastly, embracing DIY living aids in the reduction of impulse
purchases, a common challenge for many consumers. When
individuals invest time and effort into creating or repairing something,
they become more discerning about their spending habits. The process
of DIY requires planning, research, and often a significant
commitment of time, which naturally discourages mindless spending.
By cultivating a habit of thoughtful creation, people can develop a
healthier relationship with money, ultimately leading to a more
fulfilling and financially sound lifestyle.

Chapter 6: Mindful Consumerism and Ethical Shopping

The Importance of Ethical Choices

The importance of ethical choices in consumer behavior cannot be overstated, especially in today's fast-paced, marketing-driven society. Each purchase decision we make, no matter how small, contributes to a larger economic ecosystem that can either support sustainable practices or perpetuate unsustainable ones. Ethical choices often involve considering the broader implications of our spending, such as the environmental impact of products, the fair treatment of workers, and the social responsibility of companies. By prioritizing ethical options, consumers can foster a marketplace that values integrity, sustainability, and social justice.

Mindful consumerism is a critical aspect of making ethical choices. This practice encourages individuals to reflect on their purchasing habits and to be intentional about the items they bring into their lives. By distinguishing between needs and wants, consumers can avoid unnecessary purchases, which not only helps in decluttering their living spaces but also reduces financial strain. Furthermore, mindful shopping promotes a deeper connection with the products we choose, allowing us to support brands and businesses that align with our values, such as those that prioritize eco-friendly materials or fair labor practices.

Budgeting techniques can be enhanced by integrating ethical considerations into financial planning. When consumers allocate their resources toward ethical products, they often find that they are supporting higher-quality goods that may last longer and require fewer replacements. This shift in mindset can lead to long-term savings, as investing in sustainable and ethically produced items can reduce the frequency of purchases. Additionally, ethical budgeting encourages consumers to seek out alternatives, such as DIY solutions or thrifting, which not only align with a frugal approach but also promote a more sustainable lifestyle.

Reducing impulse purchases is another key area where ethical choices play a significant role. By cultivating awareness about the motivations behind spontaneous spending, individuals can learn to pause and evaluate whether a purchase aligns with their values. Strategies such as creating a shopping list, setting spending limits, or even waiting a designated period before making a purchase can help curb impulsive behaviors. This reflective practice fosters a habit of making purchasing decisions that are both financially responsible and ethically sound, leading to a more fulfilling consumer experience.

Ultimately, embracing ethical choices in spending is a powerful way to create a positive impact on both personal finances and the world at large. By choosing to support sustainable brands, engaging in mindful consumerism, and adopting budgeting techniques that prioritize ethical considerations, individuals can contribute to a more equitable and environmentally friendly marketplace. This shift not only enhances the quality of life for consumers but also encourages businesses to adopt practices that are beneficial for society and the planet, creating a ripple effect of positive change.

Researching Brands and Products

Researching brands and products is an essential skill for anyone looking to enhance their spending habits and make informed purchasing decisions. In an age where marketing tactics can easily manipulate consumer behavior, understanding how to evaluate brands and products critically can lead to smarter financial choices. This process begins with identifying the values and needs that align with your lifestyle. Whether you are embracing minimalism, practicing mindful consumerism, or seeking sustainable alternatives, knowing what you truly require can help filter out unnecessary expenditures.

One of the first steps in researching brands is to explore their histories and missions. Brands that prioritize transparency and ethical practices often provide insights into their production processes, sourcing of materials, and labor practices. This information can be invaluable, especially for consumers committed to reducing their environmental footprint or supporting ethical businesses. Websites, social media, and product reviews can provide a wealth of information about a brand's commitment to sustainability and social responsibility, enabling you to support companies that align with your values.

Product reviews play a critical role in the research process. These reviews can guide you through the experiences of other consumers, highlighting both the advantages and potential drawbacks of products. Look beyond the star ratings and consider the context of the reviews. Are users praising the durability and effectiveness, or are they complaining about hidden flaws? This detailed feedback can steer you away from impulse purchases and help you invest in items that truly add value to your life. Additionally, engaging with community forums or social media groups focused on minimalism or sustainable living can provide recommendations for products that meet ethical standards.

Comparative shopping is another powerful strategy to maximize your research efforts. By comparing similar products from different brands, you can identify not only the best price but also the best quality. Look for third-party certifications or endorsements that can signal a product's reliability, such as eco-friendly labels or fair trade certifications. Utilizing price comparison websites can also save you money by ensuring you are not overspending on a product that can be found elsewhere at a lower price. This practice not only helps you find the best deals but also encourages a thoughtful approach to purchasing.

Finally, keep in mind that research is not just about finding the best products but also about understanding your own spending habits. Reflecting on your past purchases can help identify patterns, such as impulse buys or spending on items that don't serve your true needs.

Incorporating budgeting techniques alongside your research can further reinforce mindful consumerism. By setting clear budgets for different categories and sticking to them, you can create a system that ensures every purchase is intentional. Ultimately, diligent research empowers consumers to break free from mindless spending, allowing .for a lifestyle that prioritizes quality over quantity

Building an Ethical Shopping Habit

Building an ethical shopping habit begins with awareness of the impact our purchases have on the world around us. As consumers, we wield significant power through our purchasing decisions, which can either support ethical practices or contribute to harmful industries. To cultivate an ethical shopping habit, it is essential to educate ourselves about the brands we buy from, recognize the labor practices behind products, and understand the environmental implications of our choices. By prioritizing transparency and accountability, we can make .informed decisions that align with our values

Mindful consumerism plays a crucial role in building this habit. It requires us to pause before making a purchase and reflect on whether the item is truly necessary and if it aligns with our ethical standards. This practice can be particularly beneficial in minimizing impulse purchases, a common pitfall for many shoppers. By cultivating mindfulness, we can differentiate between genuine needs and fleeting wants, ultimately leading to a more intentional and fulfilling shopping .experience

Incorporating sustainable and eco-friendly alternatives into our shopping habits is another essential aspect of ethical consumerism. Many brands now focus on sustainability, offering products made from recycled materials or those that utilize environmentally friendly production processes. Choosing these options not only supports businesses that prioritize the planet but also encourages other companies to adopt similar practices. Moreover, opting for

second-hand items through thrifting or reselling can further reduce our
ecological footprint while saving money.
Budgeting techniques can also enhance our ability to shop
ethically. By setting aside a dedicated budget for ethical and sustainable
products, we can prioritize purchases that align with our values without
overspending. This approach encourages thoughtful shopping and
allows us to invest in high-quality items that may cost more upfront but
offer long-term benefits. Furthermore, tracking our expenses can help
identify areas where we can cut back on unnecessary spending, freeing
up resources to support ethical brands.
Finally, navigating subscription services wisely can contribute to
building an ethical shopping habit. Many subscription models
prioritize convenience over conscious consumption, leading to
mindless spending. By evaluating the necessity of each subscription
and its alignment with our values, we can streamline our spending and
focus on services that promote sustainability and ethical practices. In
doing so, we not only enhance our financial health but also align our
spending habits with a commitment to a more ethical and responsible
lifestyle.

Chapter 7: Sustainable and Eco-Friendly Alternatives

Understanding Sustainability

Sustainability is an essential concept that intersects with various aspects of our daily lives, especially in the context of spending. At its core, sustainability refers to meeting our present needs without compromising the ability of future generations to meet theirs. This principle emphasizes the importance of making mindful choices that promote environmental health, social equity, and economic viability. Understanding sustainability involves recognizing the interconnectedness of these elements and how our consumption patterns can either contribute to or detract from a sustainable future.

In the realm of consumerism, the choices we make can have profound effects on the environment and society. For instance, purchasing fast fashion items may seem economical in the short term, but the long-term consequences are significant, including environmental degradation and exploitation of labor. By shifting our focus to minimalist living and decluttering, we can prioritize quality over quantity, opting for items that are durable, ethically produced, and necessary. This not only reduces waste but also fosters a more intentional lifestyle, allowing individuals to appreciate and care for the possessions they choose to keep.

Budgeting techniques play a vital role in fostering sustainability. By carefully tracking expenses and identifying areas where we can cut back on unnecessary spending, we can allocate more resources toward sustainable alternatives. For example, instead of frequenting fast-food chains, consider investing time in meal planning and cooking at home with locally sourced ingredients. This not only saves money but also supports local farmers and reduces carbon footprints associated with transporting food. Adopting frugal practices can lead to healthier eating habits while simultaneously promoting a more sustainable lifestyle.

DIY solutions for home and lifestyle can also contribute significantly to sustainability. Embracing a do-it-yourself mentality encourages creativity and resourcefulness, allowing individuals to repurpose items instead of discarding them. Whether it's upcycling furniture or creating eco-friendly cleaning products, these practices not only save money but also minimize waste and reduce reliance on mass-produced goods. This shift toward self-sufficiency fosters a deeper understanding of the resources involved in everyday products, ultimately leading to more conscious purchasing decisions.

Mindful consumerism and ethical shopping are key aspects of understanding sustainability. It involves being aware of the impact of our purchases and striving to choose brands and products that prioritize environmental stewardship and fair labor practices. This conscious approach not only enhances our personal values but also sends a clear message to manufacturers about the importance of sustainable practices. By incorporating strategies for reducing impulse purchases and navigating subscription services wisely, consumers can align their spending habits with their sustainability goals, ensuring that every dollar spent contributes positively to the world around them.

Eco-Friendly Product Options

Eco-friendly products are increasingly becoming a viable alternative for conscious consumers seeking to reduce their environmental footprint while also making prudent financial choices. As the market evolves, many eco-friendly options are not only sustainable but also budget-friendly. By choosing products made from sustainable materials, consumers can often save money in the long run. For example, reusable bags, containers, and water bottles may have a higher initial cost, but they eliminate the need for single-use items, leading to significant savings over time.

When it comes to home and lifestyle, DIY solutions can play a crucial role in promoting sustainability. Creating your own cleaning products from natural ingredients like vinegar, baking soda, and essential oils is a great way to reduce chemical exposure and cut costs. These homemade alternatives are often cheaper than their commercial counterparts and can be customized to suit individual preferences. Additionally, sourcing materials from second-hand stores or repurposing items you already own can greatly reduce waste and save money, fostering a minimalist approach to living.

Mindful consumerism is essential for addressing the challenges of impulse buying and unnecessary spending. By taking the time to research the environmental impact of products before making a purchase, consumers can make informed decisions that align with their values. Supporting brands that prioritize sustainability and ethical practices not only helps the planet but also encourages a marketplace that favors quality over quantity. This shift can lead to purchasing fewer, but more durable items, ultimately resulting in better financial management.

Budgeting techniques can also be adapted to incorporate eco-friendly practices. Setting aside a specific portion of your budget for sustainable products can incentivize mindful spending. Tracking expenses related to eco-friendly purchases versus traditional options can provide insight into long-term savings. Moreover, many eco-conscious brands offer loyalty programs or discounts for bulk purchases, allowing consumers to save while investing in products that are better for the environment.

Lastly, exploring reselling and thrifting as alternatives to new purchases can significantly contribute to both sustainability and frugality. Thrift stores and online marketplaces often provide a wide range of eco-friendly items that have been repurposed or gently used. This not only reduces waste but also allows consumers to find unique products at a fraction of the price of new items. By embracing a culture of second-hand shopping, individuals can cultivate a more sustainable lifestyle while adhering to a budget, showcasing that eco-friendly choices can align seamlessly with financial savvy.

Making Sustainable Choices in Daily Life

Making sustainable choices in daily life is essential for both personal finance and environmental stewardship. By consciously opting for eco-friendly alternatives and minimizing waste, individuals can significantly reduce their spending while contributing to a greener planet. Simple shifts in daily habits can lead to substantial savings over time. This approach aligns perfectly with the principles of minimalist living, where the focus is on quality over quantity. Embracing fewer, but more meaningful possessions not only declutters physical spaces but also simplifies financial commitments.

One effective strategy for making sustainable choices is to prioritize mindful consumerism. This involves being intentional about purchases and considering the impact of products on both the environment and personal finances. Before making a purchase, ask questions such as: Is this item truly necessary? How long will it last? Can it be repaired or repurposed? By assessing these factors, you can avoid impulse buys that often lead to clutter and wasted money. This practice not only helps in reducing spending but also fosters a deeper appreciation for the items that truly enhance your life.

Incorporating DIY solutions into your lifestyle can further support sustainable living while being budget-friendly. Many household items can be made from simple, inexpensive materials rather than purchased new. For example, creating natural cleaning products from vinegar and baking soda can save money and reduce reliance on chemical-laden commercial cleaners. Additionally, DIY projects can be a fulfilling way to engage creativity and reduce waste by repurposing materials that would otherwise be discarded. This not only promotes sustainability

but also enhances the value of your living space through personalized
.touches

Frugal meal planning is another impactful way to make sustainable choices. By planning meals around seasonal produce and bulk purchasing staples, you can minimize food waste and save money. Cooking at home with fresh ingredients not only supports local farmers but also allows for healthier eating habits. Implementing practices like batch cooking and utilizing leftovers creatively can stretch your grocery budget further while reducing the environmental
.footprint associated with food production and waste

Finally, navigating subscription services wisely can help streamline your expenses while promoting sustainability. Many subscription models encourage consumers to accumulate items they may not fully utilize. By critically evaluating each subscription and opting for services that align with your values and needs, you can prevent unnecessary spending. Additionally, consider supporting companies that prioritize ethical practices and sustainability. By choosing wisely, you can enjoy the benefits of convenient services while ensuring your spending aligns
.with your commitment to a more sustainable lifestyle

Chapter 8: Reselling and Thrifting Tips

The Benefits of Thrifting

Thrifting offers a multitude of benefits that extend beyond mere cost savings, making it an attractive option for consumers intent on making smarter financial choices. One of the most significant advantages of thrifting is the potential for substantial savings. Second-hand items, whether clothing, furniture, or household goods, are often available at a fraction of their original retail price. This reduced cost allows individuals to acquire high-quality items without straining their budgets, thereby redirecting funds toward more pressing expenses or savings goals.

In addition to financial savings, thrifting encourages a more sustainable lifestyle. By purchasing second-hand goods, consumers contribute to the reduction of waste that often results from fast fashion and disposable consumer culture. This shift in purchasing habits aligns well with the principles of mindful consumerism and ethical shopping. It fosters an appreciation for items with history and character, as well as a commitment to reducing one's carbon footprint. By choosing thrifted items over new ones, individuals can make a positive impact on the environment while enjoying unique and diverse products.

Thrifting not only promotes sustainability but also encourages creativity and resourcefulness. When exploring thrift stores, shoppers often discover unconventional items that can be repurposed or transformed through DIY projects. This aspect of thrifting allows individuals to express their creativity while also developing practical skills in upcycling and restoration. Embracing these DIY solutions can lead to a more personalized living space and a sense of accomplishment, further enhancing the overall thrifting experience.

Moreover, thrifting can serve as an effective strategy for decluttering and minimalism. Engaging with second-hand goods can inspire individuals to reevaluate their own possessions and prioritize what truly adds value to their lives. This mindset can facilitate a more intentional approach to consumption, reducing the likelihood of impulse purchases and fostering a habit of thoughtful decision-making. By embracing a minimalist lifestyle, individuals can cultivate a more organized and peaceful living environment, free from the clutter of unnecessary items.

Lastly, the benefits of thrifting extend to the community and economy. Many thrift stores are non-profit organizations that fund various social programs, meaning that every purchase made contributes to a greater cause. Shopping at these establishments supports local charities and provides job opportunities within the community. Additionally, thrifting creates a vibrant marketplace for reselling and exchanging goods, encouraging a culture of sharing and collaboration. By choosing to thrift, consumers not only enhance their own lives but also positively influence the broader community, fostering a more sustainable and interconnected world.

How to Resell Unwanted Items

Reselling unwanted items is an effective strategy for decluttering your space while also generating extra cash. The first step in this process is to assess the items you own. Begin by identifying items that you no longer use or need. This may include clothing, electronics, furniture, or household goods. A good rule of thumb is to consider whether you've used an item in the past year. If not, it might be time to let it go. Taking inventory of your belongings not only helps with decluttering but also sets the stage for a successful resale.

Once you've selected the items to sell, the next step is to determine their value. Research similar items online to see what they are selling for on platforms like eBay, Facebook Marketplace, or Poshmark. Consider the condition of your items, as well as any brand names that may increase their value. Being realistic about pricing is crucial; pricing items too high can deter potential buyers, while pricing too low can leave you feeling shortchanged. Aim for a fair price that reflects the item's condition and market demand to attract interested buyers.

To effectively market your items, high-quality photos and detailed descriptions are essential. When listing items online, take clear, well-lit photos from multiple angles. Highlight any flaws or unique features to provide potential buyers with a complete picture. In your description, include key information such as brand, size, model, and any relevant history. The more detailed and transparent you are, the more likely you are to build trust with buyers and secure a sale. Remember to be honest about the condition of your items to avoid disputes later.

Choosing the right platform for resale is equally important. There are numerous options available, each catering to different types of items and audiences. For clothing and accessories, platforms like Depop or ThredUp might be ideal. For furniture or larger items, Facebook Marketplace or Craigslist can be more effective. Additionally, consider local resale shops or consignment stores for items you prefer to sell in person. Each platform has its own set of rules and fees, so familiarize yourself with these before listing your items to ensure you are maximizing your profits.

Finally, when reselling items, practice good customer service to encourage positive interactions and repeat business. Respond promptly to inquiries and be courteous in your communications. Once a sale is finalized, ensure a smooth transaction by being punctual for meet-ups or shipping items quickly if sold online. Positive reviews and word-of-mouth can significantly boost your resale efforts, so strive to create a pleasant experience for buyers. By following these steps, you can not only declutter your home but also turn your unwanted items into cash, aligning with a more mindful and sustainable lifestyle.

Finding Hidden Gems in Thrift Stores

Finding hidden gems in thrift stores is an art that can significantly enhance your budget-conscious lifestyle while promoting mindful consumerism. Thrift stores are treasure troves filled with unique items that often carry rich histories and stories. With a little patience and an eye for detail, you can uncover quality goods at a fraction of their original price. This practice not only allows you to save money but also encourages sustainable shopping habits by giving pre-loved items a second chance.

When you enter a thrift store, it's essential to approach your search with a clear strategy. Start by setting a budget for yourself and making a list of the types of items you hope to find, whether that's clothing, home decor, or kitchenware. Familiarizing yourself with the layout of the store can also save you time. Many thrift stores categorize their items, so knowing where to look can help you focus your search. Additionally, don't be afraid to explore every corner; some of the best finds are often tucked away in unexpected places.

Condition is key when evaluating potential purchases. Inspect each item carefully for any signs of wear and tear, checking for tears, stains, or any functional issues. Many thrift stores offer items at such low prices that a small repair or a bit of cleaning can make a significant difference. Embracing a DIY mindset can turn a seemingly flawed item into a valuable addition to your home. For instance, a scratched wooden table can be sanded down and refinished, transforming it into a stunning centerpiece for your dining room.

Timing your visits to thrift stores can also enhance your chances of finding rare items. Many stores receive new donations on specific days, so visiting shortly after these drop-offs can yield fresh inventory. Additionally, consider shopping during off-peak hours when the stores are less crowded. This allows you to take your time and sift through items without feeling rushed. Building a rapport with store staff may also lead to insider tips about upcoming sales or special finds.

Finally, don't forget to embrace the thrill of the hunt. Thrift store shopping should be enjoyable rather than stressful. Keep an open mind and be willing to explore items that may not fit the conventional mold of what you're looking for. The charm of thrift stores lies in their unpredictability, and sometimes the best treasures are those you didn't know you wanted. By incorporating thrift shopping into your routine, you can cultivate a more mindful approach to consumption, ultimately leading to a more fulfilling and financially savvy lifestyle.

Chapter 9: Strategies for Reducing Impulse Purchases

The Psychology of Impulse Buying

The psychology of impulse buying is a complex interplay of emotional triggers, cognitive biases, and environmental influences that can lead consumers to make unplanned purchases. At its core, impulse buying often stems from a desire for instant gratification. When faced with a tempting product, the brain's reward system activates, releasing dopamine, which creates a feeling of pleasure. This immediate satisfaction can overshadow rational decision-making, causing shoppers to overlook their budget or long-term financial goals. Understanding this psychological mechanism is crucial for anyone looking to curb unnecessary spending and adopt more mindful consumer habits.

Cognitive biases also play a significant role in impulse buying behavior. One common bias is the scarcity effect, where limited availability of an item increases its perceived value, prompting consumers to purchase on the spot out of fear of missing out. Retailers cleverly exploit this by creating urgency through sales, countdown timers, or limited editions. This tactic can easily lead shoppers to make hasty decisions that they may later regret. Recognizing these biases can empower individuals to take a step back, assess their true needs, and resist the pressure to buy impulsively.

Environmental factors, such as store layout and marketing strategies, further contribute to impulse purchases. Retailers often design their spaces to maximize consumer engagement, placing enticing products at eye level or near checkout lines to encourage last-minute buys. Additionally, advertising techniques that evoke strong emotions or highlight social proof can create a sense of urgency or desire. By understanding how these elements influence buying behavior, individuals can become more aware of their shopping environments and develop strategies to minimize distractions and temptations.

To combat impulse buying, consumers can implement practical strategies that promote mindful spending. Creating a detailed shopping list before entering a store helps prioritize needs over wants, while setting a strict budget can serve as a financial guardrail. Furthermore, allowing a cooling-off period before making a purchase can help individuals evaluate whether the item is genuinely necessary. By incorporating these techniques into their shopping routines, consumers can significantly reduce the likelihood of falling victim to impulse buying.

Finally, embracing a minimalist lifestyle can further aid in overcoming impulse buying tendencies. By focusing on quality over quantity and valuing experiences over material possessions, individuals can cultivate a more intentional approach to consumption. This shift in mindset not only saves money but also contributes to a more sustainable and ethical way of living. Educating oneself about the environmental impact of consumerism can enhance this awareness, motivating individuals to make purchases that align with their values and contribute positively to their lives and communities.

Techniques to Pause and Reflect

Techniques to pause and reflect are essential for anyone looking to curb unnecessary spending and adopt a more mindful approach to consumerism. One effective method is the "24-Hour Rule," which encourages individuals to wait a full day before making a purchase. This simple strategy allows time for reflection and helps to differentiate between wants and needs. It often reveals that the initial excitement of a potential buy fades, making it easier to resist impulse purchases. By implementing this pause, consumers can prioritize their finances and make more informed decisions.

Another powerful technique is journaling about spending habits. Keeping a dedicated spending journal can illuminate patterns and triggers that lead to impulsive buying. By documenting purchases, along with emotions and circumstances surrounding each transaction, individuals can gain insights into their behavior. This reflection not only highlights areas for improvement but also encourages accountability. Over time, journaling can serve as a valuable tool for identifying the motivations behind spending and help to foster a more intentional relationship with money.

Mindfulness practices can also play a crucial role in pausing and reflecting before purchasing decisions. Techniques such as deep breathing, meditation, or even short walks can create space for clarity. When faced with a purchasing decision, taking a moment to breathe deeply can shift focus from the immediate urge to buy to a more thoughtful evaluation of the necessity and impact of that purchase. This practice cultivates awareness and can significantly alter the trajectory of one's spending habits, leading to more sustainable choices.

Engaging in mindful consumerism through research and education can further enhance the pause-and-reflect approach. Before making a purchase, individuals can take the time to learn about the product's environmental impact, ethical sourcing, and long-term value. This not only contributes to more conscious spending but also aligns purchases with personal values, whether they prioritize sustainability, minimalism, or ethical practices. By understanding the broader implications of their buying choices, consumers can make decisions that resonate with their ideals.

Lastly, setting specific financial goals can serve as a powerful motivator to pause and reflect. Whether it's saving for a significant purchase, paying off debt, or building an emergency fund, having clear objectives can shift the focus away from impulsive spending. Regularly reviewing these goals can reinforce the importance of mindful choices. By visualizing the benefits of reaching these targets, individuals are more likely to consider the long-term consequences of their spending habits, ultimately leading to a healthier financial lifestyle.

Creating a Shopping Plan

Creating a shopping plan is a critical step in transforming your spending habits and aligning your purchases with your values and needs. With a structured approach, you can effectively reduce unnecessary expenses and focus on what truly matters, whether it's embracing minimalist living, committing to mindful consumerism, or simply avoiding impulse purchases. A comprehensive shopping plan will not only help you save money but also cultivate a more intentional lifestyle that reflects your goals.

The first component of a successful shopping plan is to assess your current spending. Take a close look at your recent purchases to identify patterns and areas where you tend to overspend. This self-assessment can reveal habits related to impulse buys or subscription services that may no longer serve you. Consider creating a simple spreadsheet or using budgeting apps to track your expenses. By having a clear picture of where your money goes, you can establish a baseline from which to improve and make informed decisions moving forward.

Next, it's essential to establish clear goals for your shopping. Determine what you truly need and what can be classified as a want. For example, if you're focused on minimalist living, prioritize purchases that add value to your life without cluttering your space. This might mean investing in high-quality, versatile items rather than numerous cheap alternatives. Additionally, consider setting a monthly budget for discretionary spending, allowing room for fun while ensuring you remain within your financial means.

When planning your shopping list, adopt a strategic approach. Include only the items you genuinely need, and avoid adding anything that could lead to buyer's remorse. For groceries, embrace frugal meal planning by creating weekly menus that utilize similar ingredients to minimize waste and maximize savings. If you are drawn to sustainable and eco-friendly alternatives, research brands that align with your values and seek out local markets or thrift stores for unique finds. This not only supports ethical shopping but also fosters a sense of community and resourcefulness.

Finally, commit to reviewing and adjusting your shopping plan regularly. Life changes, and so do your needs and financial situations. By periodically reassessing your shopping habits, you can adapt your plan to reflect new priorities and avoid falling back into old patterns. Consider setting aside time each month to reflect on your purchases, evaluate what worked, and identify areas for improvement. This ongoing process of reflection will strengthen your financial discipline and empower you to make conscious choices that enrich your life rather than drain your wallet.

Chapter 10: Frugal Meal Planning and Cooking

Benefits of Meal Planning

Meal planning is a powerful strategy that can significantly enhance both your financial health and your overall well-being. By dedicating time to plan your meals for the week, you create a roadmap that keeps you organized, reduces food waste, and minimizes impulse purchases. When you know exactly what you need to buy and what you'll be cooking, you are less likely to make unnecessary trips to the store or succumb to the temptation of takeout, which can quickly drain your budget. This proactive approach not only saves you money but also encourages more mindful consumer habits.

One of the most immediate benefits of meal planning is its potential for reducing food waste. When meals are planned in advance, you can ensure that you are purchasing only the ingredients you will actually use, thus minimizing the likelihood of items going bad and being thrown away. This aligns with sustainable living principles by promoting a more efficient use of resources, which is essential in an age where environmental concerns are at the forefront. By being intentional about what you buy and how you cook, you contribute to a more sustainable lifestyle while also keeping your grocery bills in check.

Meal planning also fosters healthier eating habits. When you take the time to prepare meals in advance, you can incorporate a balanced mix of nutrients and avoid the temptation of unhealthy, convenience foods. This is especially beneficial for those looking to adopt a minimalist lifestyle, as it encourages you to focus on whole, unprocessed foods rather than excessive or extravagant options. Additionally, cooking at home tends to be more cost-effective than dining out or relying on pre-packaged meals, making it a smart financial choice for anyone looking to curb unnecessary spending.

Furthermore, meal planning encourages creativity in the kitchen. By dedicating time to think about your meals, you can experiment with new recipes and ingredients that you might not have considered otherwise. This creative outlet can make cooking more enjoyable and less of a chore, helping to reduce the likelihood of falling into a routine of repetitive, uninspired meals. The satisfaction of creating something from scratch not only enhances your culinary skills but can also lead to a more conscious approach to food consumption, aligning with the principles of ethical shopping and mindful consumerism.

Lastly, the skills developed through meal planning can lead to greater confidence in your overall budgeting practices. As you become more adept at managing your grocery expenses, you may find that this confidence spills over into other areas of your financial life. Learning to plan and budget effectively for meals can serve as a foundation for other budgeting techniques, whether it's managing monthly bills or navigating subscription services wisely. By honing these skills, you can cultivate a more frugal lifestyle that emphasizes thoughtful spending and sustainable practices, ultimately leading to a healthier and more fulfilling life.

Budget-Friendly Recipes

Budget-friendly recipes are not only a practical solution for saving money but also an opportunity to embrace healthier eating habits. When we prioritize meals that are cost-effective, we often find ourselves using fresh, whole ingredients that are both nourishing and satisfying. This approach encourages creativity in the kitchen, as it challenges us to make the most of what we have on hand. By focusing on meals that require minimal ingredients or utilize pantry staples, we can reduce our grocery bills while enjoying delicious, homemade dishes.

A great starting point for budget-friendly cooking is to plan meals around seasonal produce. Seasonal fruits and vegetables are generally more affordable and taste better than out-of-season options. For instance, a simple vegetable stir-fry can be made with whatever is in season, such as bell peppers, broccoli, and carrots, combined with a protein source like beans or tofu. Not only does this keep costs down, but it also supports local farmers and reduces the carbon footprint associated with transporting out-of-season produce. Incorporating these seasonal elements into your meal planning can greatly enhance both flavor and sustainability.

Another effective strategy for budget-friendly recipes is to embrace batch cooking. Preparing large quantities of meals, such as soups, stews, or casseroles, can save both time and money. These dishes often freeze well, allowing you to portion them out for later use. This not only minimizes food waste but also helps you avoid the temptation of ordering takeout on busy nights. When you have a homemade meal ready to go in the freezer, you can confidently say no to impulse purchases and expensive convenience foods.

In addition to batch cooking, consider utilizing versatile ingredients that can be transformed into multiple meals. Items like rice, pasta, and legumes can serve as the base for a variety of dishes throughout the week. For example, a pot of rice can be turned into stir-fried rice, rice salads, or stuffed peppers. This flexibility allows you to stretch your grocery budget further while reducing the monotony of repeated meals. By thinking creatively about how to use each ingredient, you can create a diverse menu without overspending.

Lastly, don't underestimate the power of simple recipes that require minimal effort yet deliver maximum flavor. Dishes like roasted vegetables, grain bowls, or simple salads can be both satisfying and economical. By focusing on whole ingredients and easy cooking methods, you can enjoy nutritious meals without the need for elaborate recipes or expensive components. This approach aligns well with a minimalist lifestyle, emphasizing the importance of quality over quantity while promoting mindful consumerism in your food choices.

By adopting budget-friendly recipes, you can nourish your body and
wallet simultaneously.

Reducing Food Waste

Reducing food waste is an essential practice that not only contributes
to financial savings but also promotes a more sustainable lifestyle. In
households across the globe, an alarming amount of food is discarded
each year, leading to significant financial losses and environmental
impacts. By understanding the causes of food waste and implementing
practical strategies, everyone can take steps to minimize this waste,
ultimately leading to smarter spending and a more mindful approach
to consumption.

One of the primary reasons for food waste is poor meal planning.
Many individuals and families buy groceries without a clear plan,
resulting in excess items that often spoil before they can be used. By
creating a weekly meal plan and sticking to a shopping list, you can
ensure that you only purchase what you need. This not only helps in
reducing waste but also encourages the preparation of healthier meals
at home, thus minimizing reliance on takeout and processed foods,
which can be more expensive.

Another effective strategy for reducing food waste is to embrace
proper food storage techniques. Understanding how to store fruits,
vegetables, dairy, and meats can significantly extend their shelf life. For
example, keeping produce in the right humidity levels and temperature
can prevent premature spoilage. Additionally, labeling leftovers with
dates can help remind you to consume them before they go bad. Taking
the time to learn about food preservation methods, such as freezing,
can also allow you to save surplus food and minimize waste.

Mindful consumption is not just about what you buy, but also
about how you use the products you purchase. Being conscious of
portion sizes can help prevent over-preparation and ensure that meals
are enjoyed without leftovers going to waste. Practicing "first in, first

out" in your pantry can also encourage the use of older items, preventing them from being forgotten and ultimately discarded. This approach also ties into budgeting techniques, as using what you already .have can save money that would otherwise be spent on new groceries Lastly, consider the benefits of sharing or donating excess food. If you find yourself with surplus items that you know you won't use, sharing with friends, family, or local food banks can help combat food waste while fostering a sense of community. Engaging in local initiatives that focus on food recovery can also connect you with others who are passionate about reducing waste. By adopting these practices, you can not only save money but also contribute to a larger movement .towards mindful consumerism and sustainable living

Chapter 11: Navigating Subscription Services Wisely

Evaluating the Value of Subscriptions

Evaluating the value of subscriptions is essential in a world where monthly fees can silently drain your finances. Many people sign up for various subscription services, from streaming platforms to meal kits, without fully assessing their worth. To avoid wasting money, start by reviewing each subscription's actual usage and benefits. Consider how often you use the service and whether it truly enhances your life. For example, if you rarely watch shows on a streaming service, it may be time to cancel that subscription and redirect those funds toward something more valuable.

Next, compare the costs of subscription services against alternatives. Often, a subscription might seem like a good deal compared to a single purchase, but this isn't always the case. For instance, if you subscribe to a monthly book service but only read one book a month, it may be more cost-effective to buy the books individually. Similarly, with meal kit subscriptions, evaluate whether grocery shopping and meal prep would actually save you money and provide more flexibility in your diet. Taking the time to weigh these options can lead to significant savings.

Another critical factor in evaluating subscription value is understanding the potential for hidden costs. Some services may lure you in with low introductory prices but then increase fees over time, or they may have additional charges for premium features. It's vital to read the fine print and understand the full financial commitment. Additionally, consider whether the subscription includes features that you may not use or need. If you're paying for extras that you seldom utilize, it's worth reconsidering the service altogether.

Mindful consumption is a vital part of evaluating subscriptions.
Reflect on what you genuinely enjoy and what aligns with your
lifestyle. If a subscription feels more like a burden than a benefit, it is
likely not worth keeping. Embracing minimalist living encourages you
to prioritize experiences and services that truly enhance your quality of
life. By being intentional about your subscriptions, you can cultivate a
more meaningful and financially sound lifestyle.

Lastly, consider the environmental impact of your subscriptions.
Sustainable and eco-friendly alternatives are becoming increasingly
available, and many people are seeking ways to support ethical
businesses. When evaluating subscriptions, assess whether they align
with your values regarding sustainability and responsible consumption.
This approach not only helps you save money but also ensures that your
spending reflects your principles, promoting a healthier planet and a
more fulfilling lifestyle.

Choosing the Right Subscriptions for You

Choosing the right subscriptions can significantly impact your budget
and overall spending habits. With an increasing number of
subscription services available, it's essential to evaluate your needs and
lifestyle before committing. Begin by assessing what subscriptions you
currently have and determining their value. Are you frequently using
them, or have they become an unnecessary drain on your finances?
Keep in mind that subscriptions should enhance your life, not
complicate it. By taking a close look at your usage patterns, you can
identify which services are worth the investment and which can be
eliminated.

When considering new subscriptions, prioritize those that align
with your interests and values. For example, if you embrace minimalist
living, seek out services that offer quality over quantity. A subscription
that provides access to curated, high-quality items or experiences may
be more beneficial than one that overwhelms you with choices.

Similarly, if you are focused on sustainability, look for subscriptions that promote eco-friendly practices or support ethical brands. By choosing subscriptions that resonate with your lifestyle, you can ensure that your spending aligns with your principles and enhances your well-being.

Budgeting for subscriptions is crucial to avoid overspending. Treat subscriptions like fixed monthly expenses and include them in your budget plan. This approach helps you remain mindful of your financial commitments and encourages you to think critically about each service's worth. Consider setting a limit on how much you are willing to spend on subscriptions each month. By doing this, you can prioritize the services that provide the most value and eliminate those that do not contribute positively to your life.

Impulse purchases often plague consumers, especially with the ease of subscribing online. To combat this, implement a waiting period before committing to new subscriptions. For example, if you find a service that interests you, wait for a week before signing up. This pause allows you to evaluate whether the subscription is truly necessary and prevents you from making hasty decisions. Additionally, consider exploring free trials to test out services before fully committing. This strategy can help you make informed choices and reduce the likelihood of wasting money on subscriptions that do not meet your expectations.

Lastly, consider the potential for reselling or sharing subscriptions. Many services allow multiple users, which can be an opportunity to split costs with friends or family. Alternatively, if you have subscriptions that you no longer use, explore reselling options to recoup some of your expenses. Platforms dedicated to buying and selling unused subscriptions can help you recover funds and minimize waste. By adopting a thoughtful approach to subscription choices, you can cultivate a spending strategy that supports your goals of mindful consumerism and financial health.

Canceling Unused Services

Canceling unused services is an essential step towards reclaiming your finances and ensuring that your hard-earned money is not wasted on things you do not use or need. Many individuals find themselves subscribed to multiple services, from streaming platforms to gym memberships, that they hardly utilize. These subscriptions can quietly drain your budget month after month, leading to a significant cumulative expense over time. By taking a closer look at these services and assessing their value in your life, you can make informed decisions that benefit your financial situation.

Begin by conducting a thorough audit of all your subscriptions and services. Create a list that includes everything you're currently paying for, along with the cost and the frequency of use. This can include digital services such as Netflix, Spotify, and cloud storage, as well as physical memberships like gyms or clubs. Once you have a clear view of your commitments, identify which services you actively use and which ones have become unnecessary. This exercise often reveals surprising insights about how much you are actually spending on services that add little to no value to your life.

After identifying the unused services, it is crucial to evaluate whether they can be canceled without significant repercussions. Consider the terms of service for each subscription; some may have cancellation fees or require a notice period. Make a list of the services you plan to cancel and follow up promptly to ensure that your cancellations are processed correctly. Many companies make the cancellation process intentionally difficult, so be prepared to navigate through customer service channels if necessary. Document your cancellations to keep track of what has been officially terminated.

In addition to freeing up cash, canceling unused services can streamline your life, which aligns closely with minimalist living and decluttering principles. When you no longer have to manage multiple subscriptions, you can focus on the essentials that truly enhance your lifestyle. This reduction not only simplifies your finances but can also lead to a more mindful approach to consumption. When you have fewer distractions from unnecessary services, you can redirect your energy towards activities that bring genuine joy and fulfillment.

Finally, consider adopting a proactive approach to subscription services in the future. Be mindful of signing up for new services, and always ask yourself if it is something you will use regularly. Look for alternatives that offer flexibility, such as pay-per-use models or family plans that can be shared among friends or relatives. This mindful consumerism can help you avoid the trap of impulse purchases and ensure that your spending aligns with your values. By being intentional about your subscriptions and regularly reviewing your expenditures, you can cultivate a healthier financial habit that supports both your budget and your lifestyle aspirations.

Chapter 12: Investing in Experiences Over Material Goods

In our consumer-driven world, it's easy to fall into the trap of believing that material goods bring happiness and fulfillment. The shiny new car, the latest smartphone, or the trendy wardrobe update can seem like pathways to contentment. However, research consistently shows that investing in experiences, rather than accumulating possessions, leads to greater and longer-lasting happiness. Experiences enrich our lives in ways that material things cannot, providing memories, personal growth, and a deeper sense of satisfaction.

The Science Behind Experience-Based Spending

Studies in the field of psychology suggest that the joy we derive from material goods is fleeting. The concept of "hedonic adaptation" explains that we quickly get used to new possessions, and they lose their initial appeal. That brand-new car might excite you for a few weeks, but soon it becomes just another part of your daily routine. In contrast, experiences—whether it's a vacation, a concert, or a day spent with loved ones—create lasting memories that continue to bring joy long after the event is over.

Psychologist Dr. Thomas Gilovich, who has studied the relationship between money and happiness, concludes that experiences are a better investment than material things because they become part of our identity. We are the sum of our experiences, not the objects we own. A trip to a new country, an outdoor adventure, or even attending a cooking class shapes who we are, provides us with stories to share, and helps us grow in meaningful ways.

Building Connections Through Experiences

One of the most valuable aspects of investing in experiences is the opportunity to build and strengthen relationships. Experiences often involve other people, whether it's friends, family, or even strangers we meet along the way. Sharing these moments can lead to deeper .connections and create bonds that material goods simply cannot offer For example, a family vacation might cost the same as a new television, but the value of the time spent together, the shared laughter, and the new experiences will outlast any temporary satisfaction a new gadget could bring. Similarly, going to a concert with friends or participating in a group activity can foster a sense of community and .belonging, which is critical for emotional well-being

Experiences Contribute to Personal Growth

Beyond creating memories and connections, experiences also contribute to personal growth. Traveling to new places exposes you to different cultures and perspectives, broadening your understanding of the world. Engaging in new hobbies or trying something outside your comfort zone challenges you in ways that material goods cannot. These experiences help you develop new skills, boost your confidence, and .open the door to personal discovery

Moreover, experiences provide opportunities for self-reflection. Whether you're hiking in the mountains or spending a quiet afternoon at an art exhibit, these moments often give you the mental space to think about your goals, passions, and purpose in life. Material .possessions, on the other hand, rarely offer this level of introspection

Creating Lasting Happiness

When you invest in experiences, you're investing in memories that will last a lifetime. These memories become part of your personal narrative and can be revisited anytime you reflect on them. They also often become more valuable over time. Unlike material possessions, which depreciate and can be forgotten or discarded, the experiences you accumulate grow in sentimental value.

For example, a weekend getaway with friends might cost the same as buying a new outfit. Over time, the outfit may wear out or go out of style, but the memories of the trip will only grow richer as you look back on them. The shared stories and laughter from that weekend will bring a smile to your face long after the initial investment.

Practical Steps for Shifting Your Spending

If you want to make the shift toward investing in experiences over material goods, start by evaluating where your money goes. Take a look at your budget and identify areas where you might be overspending on items that don't bring long-term joy. Could that money be better spent on an experience that will enrich your life?

Consider setting aside a portion of your income specifically for experiences. Whether it's a small monthly budget for local activities or saving up for a larger event like a vacation, being intentional about experience-based spending can help you cultivate a richer, more fulfilling life.

Remember, the goal is not to completely eliminate material spending but to prioritize experiences that align with your values and passions. By investing in experiences, you're choosing to spend your money in ways that nurture your soul, strengthen your relationships, and create lasting happiness.

Ultimately, the value of experiences lies in their ability to enrich your life in meaningful ways that go beyond the superficial appeal of possessions. When you invest in experiences, you're investing in yourself and the memories that will sustain your happiness for years to come.

Chapter 13: Mastering Financial Tracking Tools

In the quest to quit wasting cash and develop smart spending habits, understanding where your money goes is essential. One of the most effective ways to take control of your finances is by using financial tracking tools. These tools provide valuable insights into your spending habits, help you set and stick to budgets, and give you the confidence to make informed financial decisions.

Gone are the days when financial tracking involved tedious manual bookkeeping. Today, there are numerous apps, software programs, and even built-in features on smartphones that make it easier than ever to monitor your spending, savings, and overall financial health. In this chapter, we'll explore how to effectively use financial tracking tools, the benefits of automating your finances, and how to choose the best platform for your needs.

The Power of Financial Tracking

Financial tracking tools provide transparency, showing you exactly where your money is going. This information can be an eye-opener, especially if you've never closely monitored your spending before. When you start to see the patterns—like how much you spend on eating out, impulse buys, or unused subscriptions—you're better equipped to make changes that will help you save.

Tracking your finances allows you to set specific goals, such as saving for a vacation, paying off debt, or building an emergency fund. By knowing exactly how much money is coming in and going out each month, you can create realistic plans that align with your financial priorities. Whether your goal is to cut back on unnecessary spending or

to allocate more money toward savings, financial tracking gives you the
clarity to make intentional choices.

Popular Financial Tracking Tools

There are countless financial tracking tools available, ranging from simple budgeting apps to comprehensive financial management platforms. Here are a few popular options to consider:

1. **Mint**: One of the most widely used personal finance apps, Mint connects directly to your bank accounts, credit cards, and investment accounts to give you a real-time overview of your finances. It automatically categorizes your transactions, helping you see how much you're spending in different areas like groceries, entertainment, or utilities. Mint also allows you to set budgets and will send alerts when you're approaching your spending limits.

2. **YNAB (You Need A Budget)**: This app is designed to help you take a proactive approach to budgeting. YNAB encourages you to give every dollar a purpose, meaning you allocate your income to specific categories like rent, savings, or debt repayment. It's a powerful tool for users who want to gain more control over their spending and plan for the future.

3. **Personal Capital**: For those who want a more comprehensive view of their finances, Personal Capital is a great option. In addition to tracking spending, it also provides investment tracking and retirement planning tools. This platform is ideal for individuals looking to manage both their day-to-day expenses and their long-term financial goals.

4. **Goodbudget**: If you prefer an envelope-based budgeting system, Goodbudget is a digital solution that allows you to allocate your money into virtual envelopes for various

spending categories. This app is simple and effective for those who want to adopt a cash-based approach to budgeting without the need for actual envelopes.

5. **Spreadsheets**: For those who prefer a more hands-on approach, creating a custom spreadsheet using programs like Microsoft Excel or Google Sheets can be a powerful way to track finances. While this method requires more manual input, it allows for complete customization and control over how you track your income and expenses.

The Benefits of Automating Your Finances

One of the major advantages of using financial tracking tools is the ability to automate your finances. Automation can help you stay on top of bills, save regularly, and avoid the temptation of overspending. Here are a few ways to leverage automation for better financial management:

1. **Automated Bill Payments**: Setting up automatic payments for recurring bills ensures you never miss a due date, helping you avoid late fees and protect your credit score. Most banks and credit cards offer automatic payment options, making it easy to streamline your bill-paying process.

2. **Automatic Savings Transfers**: Many financial tracking tools allow you to set up automatic transfers from your checking account to a savings account. By automating your savings, you can ensure that you're consistently setting aside money for future goals without having to think about it.

3. **Investment Contributions**: If you're focused on building wealth through investing, automating your contributions to retirement accounts or investment portfolios can be a powerful strategy. Many financial platforms, such as Personal Capital or brokerage accounts, allow you to set up recurring

.transfers into your investments

Subscription Management: Tracking tools like Truebill help.4 identify recurring subscription services you might not be aware of or no longer need. This can be a quick way to free up extra cash by canceling unused subscriptions, helping you stay .mindful of where your money is going

Choosing the Right Tool for You

With so many financial tracking tools available, it's important to choose one that fits your needs and preferences. Here are a few factors :to consider when selecting the best platform for you

Ease of Use: Look for a tool with an intuitive interface that.1 makes tracking your finances simple. If an app is too .complicated, you may be less likely to use it regularly

Customization Options: Some people prefer a high level of.2 customization, while others want a tool that does most of the work for them. Consider how much control you want over categorizing expenses, setting budgets, and tracking specific .financial goals

Security: Since financial tracking tools connect to your bank.3 accounts and personal information, it's crucial to choose a platform with strong security features. Look for tools that offer encryption, two-factor authentication, and other .safeguards to protect your data

Cost: Many financial tracking tools offer free versions with.4 basic features, while others require a subscription for more advanced tools. Consider whether the features of a paid .service are worth the cost for your financial situation

Taking Control of Your Financial Future

Mastering financial tracking tools is a crucial step in your journey toward smarter spending. By gaining clarity on where your money is going, you'll be able to make more intentional decisions that align with your goals. Whether you want to cut unnecessary spending, boost your savings, or manage debt, the insights gained from tracking your finances can be transformative. With the right tools and strategies in place, you can quit wasting cash and create a financial plan that supports your aspirations and long-term financial well-being.

Chapter 14: Cutting Back on Luxuries Without Feeling Deprived

When working toward better financial habits, one of the most challenging aspects is cutting back on luxury spending. Whether it's dining at fancy restaurants, shopping for the latest fashion trends, or indulging in expensive hobbies, luxury purchases can quickly drain your bank account. But cutting back on these indulgences doesn't have to mean sacrificing your quality of life. In fact, with the right mindset and strategies, you can reduce your luxury spending without feeling deprived.

In this chapter, we'll explore how to identify and prioritize your luxury expenses, implement practical ways to cut back, and shift your perspective on what truly adds value to your life.

Understanding Your Luxury Spending Habits

Before you can start cutting back, it's important to understand where your luxury spending is going. Take a moment to reflect on the items and experiences you splurge on. Are they impulse purchases, or are they things you genuinely enjoy and find worthwhile? Understanding the difference between "wants" and "needs" is key to making more mindful financial decisions.

Start by analyzing your recent purchases. You may be surprised at how often you spend on non-essentials like gourmet coffee, entertainment subscriptions, or frequent vacations. Ask yourself: Do these purchases bring long-term satisfaction, or are they short-lived pleasures?

The goal is not to eliminate all luxury spending but to be more intentional about where you allocate your money. Once you're clear on which luxuries matter most to you, you can start cutting back in areas that don't add significant value.

Prioritizing What Matters Most

The concept of luxury is subjective—what feels indulgent to one person might be a necessity to another. The key to cutting back on luxuries without feeling deprived is to prioritize the luxuries that bring you the most joy and fulfillment. This approach is sometimes referred to as "value-based spending," where you focus your money on things that truly matter to you, while cutting out the ones that don't. For example, if you absolutely love traveling, it might make sense to allocate a portion of your budget for an annual trip, while cutting back on other luxuries like expensive dinners or designer clothes. The idea is to strike a balance that aligns with your personal values and financial goals.

To help with prioritization, ask yourself the following questions:

● *Does this purchase enhance my well-being or bring me lasting happiness?*
● *Is there a less expensive alternative that could provide the same enjoyment?*
● *How often do I indulge in this luxury, and would cutting back create a significant difference in my financial situation?*

By prioritizing what matters most, you can make room for the luxuries that enrich your life without overspending on things that don't.

Finding Affordable Alternatives

One of the easiest ways to cut back on luxury spending is to find more affordable alternatives that still provide a sense of indulgence. You don't have to completely give up the things you love—you just need to get creative with how you enjoy them.

Here are some ideas for scaling back luxuries without sacrificing enjoyment:

● **Dining out**: Instead of dining at high-end restaurants, opt for casual dining or trying out new recipes at home. Hosting a dinner party with friends can also create a memorable experience without the hefty price tag.

● **Travel**: Consider exploring local destinations or booking off-season travel to save on accommodation and airfare. Staycations or weekend getaways can also provide a refreshing break without the cost of an international trip.

● **Shopping**: Rather than buying designer brands at full price, look for sales, discounts, or shop second-hand. Thrift stores, consignment shops, and online resale platforms often offer luxury items at a fraction of the cost.

● **Entertainment**: Instead of expensive concert tickets or theater outings, consider free or low-cost events in your community. Many cities offer free concerts, outdoor movie screenings, or cultural festivals that provide entertainment without the high price.

These alternatives allow you to continue enjoying the luxuries you love, while saving money and reducing the impact on your finances.

Shifting Your Perspective on Luxury

At the heart of cutting back on luxuries without feeling deprived is a mindset shift. Often, we associate luxury with happiness, believing that owning the latest gadgets or indulging in high-end experiences will bring us fulfillment. However, true contentment comes from appreciating what you already have and finding joy in simple pleasures. Consider adopting a "gratitude mindset," where you focus on what you're grateful for, rather than constantly seeking out the next luxury.

Practicing gratitude can help you realize that many of the things you already enjoy in life—whether it's a cup of coffee at home, a walk in nature, or quality time with loved ones—are luxuries in their own right. Additionally, focusing on experiences over material goods (as discussed in Chapter 12) can help you cultivate a sense of satisfaction that doesn't rely on constant consumption. Experiences, especially those shared with others, tend to create longer-lasting happiness compared to material possessions.

Conclusion: Balance is Key

Cutting back on luxury spending doesn't have to feel like deprivation. By understanding your spending habits, prioritizing what matters most, and finding affordable alternatives, you can still enjoy life's indulgences without compromising your financial goals. With a little mindfulness and a shift in perspective, you'll find that true luxury is not about how much you spend, but how you appreciate and enjoy what you already have.

This balanced approach to luxury spending will not only improve your finances but also enhance your overall well-being, as you learn to focus on what truly brings joy and fulfillment.

Chapter 15: Managing Social Pressure to Spend

In today's world, social pressure to spend money can be overwhelming. From advertisements constantly flashing on your screen to friends inviting you to expensive outings, there's always something or someone encouraging you to open your wallet. Managing this pressure, while staying true to your financial goals, can be difficult, especially when it feels like everyone around you is spending freely. But the truth is, learning how to navigate social pressure is an essential part of developing smart spending habits.

In this chapter, we'll explore strategies to resist social pressure, stay focused on your financial priorities, and still enjoy your social life without breaking the bank.

The Influence of Social Media and Advertising

Social media has dramatically changed the way we perceive spending. Every time you scroll through your feed, you're bombarded with images of luxurious vacations, designer clothes, and extravagant lifestyles. It's easy to feel like you're falling behind if you're not constantly keeping up with these trends. But it's important to remember that social media often presents a filtered version of reality—most people aren't sharing their struggles, only their successes.

Advertising works in a similar way, tapping into our emotions to make us feel like we need a particular product or experience to be happy or successful. From the latest smartphone to the hottest new restaurant in town, marketing is designed to create a sense of urgency and FOMO (fear of missing out).

To combat these influences, try these strategies:

Limit your exposure: Cut down on social media usage or ●
unfollow accounts that make you feel pressured to spend. Instead,
follow accounts that inspire financial mindfulness or provide valuable
content on budgeting, saving, and living a fulfilling life.
Be mindful of ads: Be conscious of the fact that advertisements ●
are designed to make you spend. When you see an ad, take a moment to
question whether you really need the product or if you're being swayed
by clever marketing tactics.
Set your own trends: Instead of comparing yourself to others, ●
focus on your own financial goals. Remind yourself that it's okay to
prioritize saving over spending on trends that may be fleeting.

Handling Social Situations and Peer Pressure

Social pressure doesn't just come from the media—it can also come
from friends, family, and coworkers. You might feel obligated to spend
money on dinners out, gifts, or group activities because you don't want
to disappoint others or feel left out. However, managing your finances
doesn't mean you have to say no to every social event—it just means
finding a balance.
Here are some ways to navigate social situations without
overspending:
Be honest about your financial goals: It's okay to share with ●
friends or family that you're working on saving money or cutting back
on unnecessary spending. You don't need to go into detail, but being
upfront can help them understand your choices.
Suggest alternatives: If an expensive night out doesn't fit into ●
your budget, suggest more affordable options like a potluck dinner at
home, a picnic in the park, or a movie night. Your friends might even
appreciate the change of pace.
Set boundaries: If you find yourself consistently pressured to ●
spend beyond your means, it's important to set personal boundaries.

Politely decline invitations that don't align with your financial goals, and don't feel guilty about prioritizing your own well-being.
• **Split costs**: In group settings, don't be afraid to suggest splitting costs evenly or asking if people can pay their share upfront. This can prevent awkward situations where you're stuck covering a larger portion of the bill.

The Psychology of Keeping Up with Others

One of the biggest drivers of social pressure to spend is the desire to keep up with others. Whether it's keeping up with the latest trends, gadgets, or experiences, the fear of missing out can lead to reckless spending. This phenomenon, often called "keeping up with the Joneses," can trap you in a cycle of overspending to maintain appearances.

To break free from this mindset:
• **Redefine success**: Success is personal, and it doesn't have to be tied to material possessions or extravagant experiences. Define what success means for you—whether it's financial freedom, achieving personal goals, or creating meaningful relationships—and let that guide your decisions.
• **Practice contentment**: Instead of focusing on what you don't have, appreciate what you do. Practicing gratitude can shift your mindset from scarcity to abundance, making it easier to resist the pressure to buy things just because others have them.
• **Celebrate financial wins**: Share your financial achievements with supportive friends or communities that encourage smart money habits. Celebrating milestones, like paying off debt or reaching a savings goal, can help reinforce the importance of sticking to your financial plan.

Staying True to Your Financial Priorities

It's easy to get caught up in the moment and spend money you didn't plan to, especially when you're with friends or family. However, staying true to your financial priorities is crucial for long-term success. The key is finding balance—enjoying social interactions without sacrificing your financial health.

Here are some final tips for staying focused:

● **Create a budget for socializing:** Designate a portion of your monthly budget for social activities, so you can participate in events without feeling guilty or overspending.

● **Practice delayed gratification:** Before making a purchase, especially one driven by social pressure, give yourself time to think it over. Waiting a few days can help you decide if the expense is really worth it.

● **Focus on experiences, not things:** Social gatherings don't have to revolve around spending money. Focus on creating memories and shared experiences rather than equating fun with spending.

Conclusion: Empower Yourself with Financial Confidence

Navigating social pressure to spend is a skill that takes practice. By staying true to your values, setting boundaries, and focusing on what matters most to you, you'll be able to enjoy social interactions without the burden of financial stress. The more confident you become in managing your money, the easier it will be to resist external pressures and stay on the path toward financial freedom.

Remember, true wealth isn't about keeping up with others—it's about creating a life that aligns with your personal goals and financial well-being.

Chapter 16: Embracing Delayed Gratification

In today's fast-paced, consumer-driven society, the concept of waiting for what we want can feel antiquated. With credit cards, online shopping, and instant deliveries, we've been conditioned to expect immediate satisfaction. However, the practice of delayed gratification—the ability to resist the temptation for an immediate reward in favor of a greater one later—can be one of the most powerful tools in developing smart financial habits.

This chapter explores how embracing delayed gratification can significantly improve your spending habits, increase your financial security, and help you achieve long-term goals. It's not about depriving yourself, but rather about making more thoughtful and rewarding decisions with your money.

Why Delayed Gratification Matters

At its core, delayed gratification is about self-control and planning for the future. It's the ability to say "no" to impulsive spending in order to say "yes" to something that will provide greater value down the road. Whether you're saving for a large purchase, working toward financial freedom, or simply trying to reduce unnecessary expenses, practicing delayed gratification can help you make choices that align with your goals.

Here's why delayed gratification is so important for smart spending:

- **Prevents impulse purchases**: When you wait before buying something, you give yourself time to assess whether you truly need or want it. This helps you avoid unnecessary purchases driven by fleeting desires or emotions.

Increases savings: By resisting the urge to spend immediately, ●
you can set aside more money for savings or investments, ultimately
building a stronger financial foundation.

Boosts long-term satisfaction: Studies show that people who ●
practice delayed gratification often experience greater satisfaction when
they do make purchases because they've taken the time to ensure it
aligns with their values and needs.

Develops discipline: Delaying gratification requires ●
self-discipline, which is essential for achieving bigger financial goals
like paying off debt, saving for a home, or planning for retirement.

Practical Ways to Practice Delayed Gratification

While the concept of delayed gratification might seem simple, it can
be challenging to put into practice, especially in a world designed for
convenience and instant results. The good news is that it's a skill you
can develop over time with small, intentional steps.

Here are some practical strategies to help you embrace delayed
gratification in your spending habits:

Create a cooling-off period: For non-essential purchases, ●
impose a waiting period before buying. This could be 24 hours, a week,
or even a month depending on the size of the purchase. Use this time to
think about whether the item is something you truly need or if it's just
a passing want.

Set long-term financial goals: Having clear, concrete financial ●
goals makes it easier to delay gratification because you know what
you're working toward. Whether it's saving for a vacation, an
emergency fund, or retirement, keep your goals in mind when deciding
whether to spend or save.

Break down large purchases: If you're planning to make a big ●
purchase, break it down into smaller savings goals. For example, instead
of using credit to buy a new phone immediately, save a specific amount

each month until you can pay for it in full. Not only will this prevent you from accumulating debt, but it will also make the purchase more satisfying.

● **Reward yourself mindfully**: Delaying gratification doesn't mean never treating yourself. It means being intentional about when and how you reward yourself. Set small milestones along your financial journey and allow yourself a reward that fits within your budget. This could be something like a nice dinner out after reaching a savings goal or a day trip when you've paid off a credit card balance.

● **Focus on experiences, not things**: Often, the things we buy provide short-lived satisfaction, whereas experiences can offer lasting fulfillment. Instead of spending money on material items that may lose their appeal, focus on investing in experiences like travel, learning new skills, or spending time with loved ones.

Overcoming the Challenges of Instant Gratification

While delayed gratification has clear benefits, it can be difficult to resist the pull of instant gratification, especially when it's so deeply ingrained in our daily lives. Whether it's the temptation of an online sale or the convenience of same-day delivery, we're constantly surrounded by opportunities to spend money impulsively.

Here's how to overcome common challenges associated with instant gratification:

● **Identify triggers**: Pay attention to situations or emotions that lead you to spend impulsively. Are you more likely to shop when you're stressed, bored, or influenced by others? Once you identify these triggers, you can work on strategies to manage them, such as finding alternative ways to relieve stress or setting limits on how much time you spend browsing online stores.

● **Practice mindful spending**: When faced with a purchasing decision, take a moment to reflect on why you want to buy the item. Is it something you truly need, or are you seeking immediate pleasure or distraction? By practicing mindfulness, you can make more conscious spending choices and avoid impulse buys.

● **Visualize the long-term benefits**: When you're tempted to spend impulsively, remind yourself of the long-term benefits of waiting. Visualize the progress you'll make toward your financial goals if you hold off on the purchase. This mental exercise can help strengthen your resolve to delay gratification.

The Rewards of Delayed Gratification

Although delayed gratification requires patience and discipline, the rewards are well worth the effort. By choosing to wait, you're not just saving money—you're investing in a more secure financial future, reducing stress, and gaining greater control over your spending habits. Here are some of the key rewards of embracing delayed gratification:

● **Increased financial freedom**: When you resist the urge to spend impulsively, you free up more money for savings, investments, and paying off debt. This leads to greater financial security and the ability to make choices that align with your values, rather than being driven by short-term desires.

● **More meaningful purchases**: When you take the time to carefully consider your purchases, the items or experiences you choose to invest in will likely hold more meaning and provide greater satisfaction.

● **Stronger self-discipline**: Each time you practice delayed gratification, you strengthen your ability to control your spending and stay focused on your financial goals. Over time, this discipline will extend to other areas of your life, making it easier to achieve success in both your personal and financial endeavors.

Conclusion: The Long-Term Benefits of Waiting

Embracing delayed gratification is about understanding that good things often come to those who wait. By making more intentional decisions with your money, you'll not only improve your financial situation but also experience greater satisfaction from the things you do choose to invest in.

Remember, delayed gratification is a skill that takes practice. Start small by applying the principles in your day-to-day spending, and over time, you'll develop the discipline needed to make smarter financial decisions that will benefit you in the long run.

Chapter 17: Financial Literacy for a Smarter Future

In the pursuit of smart spending, one often-overlooked aspect is the importance of financial literacy. Financial literacy goes beyond just knowing how to budget or save; it encompasses a deeper understanding of how money works, how to grow it, and how to make informed decisions that secure your financial future. Developing a solid foundation of financial knowledge will help you make choices that align with your long-term goals, avoid common financial pitfalls, and ultimately lead to a more secure and stress-free relationship with money.

This chapter explores why financial literacy is essential for smart spending, how to improve your own financial knowledge, and practical steps you can take to make better financial decisions.

Why Financial Literacy Matters

Financial literacy is the ability to understand and effectively use various financial skills, including personal financial management, budgeting, and investing. While many people know the basics of saving money or avoiding debt, financial literacy gives you the tools to make smarter, more informed decisions about every aspect of your finances.

Here are some reasons why financial literacy is crucial for smart spending:

• **Improved decision-making**: When you have a good grasp of financial concepts like interest rates, investments, and inflation, you're better equipped to make decisions that benefit your financial well-being.

Debt management: Understanding how credit works, how to ●
manage debt, and the long-term effects of loans or credit card interest
can prevent you from falling into financial traps.
Goal setting: Financial literacy helps you set realistic, achievable ●
financial goals, whether it's saving for a down payment on a home,
planning for retirement, or building an emergency fund.
Wealth-building opportunities: With financial literacy, you're ●
more likely to recognize opportunities for growing your wealth, such as
smart investments, building passive income streams, or starting a side
business.
Confidence and empowerment: The more you understand ●
about your finances, the more confident and empowered you'll feel
to make choices that serve your best interests, rather than relying on
others to make decisions for you.

Key Areas of Financial Literacy

To improve your financial literacy, it's important to focus on several
key areas. Each of these components plays a crucial role in helping you
manage your money wisely and avoid financial setbacks.

1. **Budgeting**: A well-designed budget is the foundation of
good financial management. Learn how to track your income
and expenses, prioritize your spending, and adjust your
budget as your financial situation changes. Understanding
the difference between fixed and variable expenses and being
aware of discretionary versus non-discretionary spending will
help you make smarter choices.
2. **Saving and Investing**: Learn the importance of saving for
short-term and long-term goals, such as an emergency fund,
retirement, or a significant purchase. Basic investing
knowledge, such as how stocks, bonds, and mutual funds

work, can help you make more informed choices when
.growing your wealth
Debt Management: Credit cards, loans, and mortgages are.3
common financial tools, but they can become burdensome if
not managed properly. Understand how interest works, the
difference between good and bad debt, and strategies for
paying down debt efficiently. Knowledge of how credit scores
.impact your financial future is also crucial
Taxes: Taxes can seem complicated, but understanding the.4
basics of how they're calculated, what deductions or credits
you may be eligible for, and how to file your taxes correctly
.can save you money in the long run
Retirement Planning: Even if retirement feels far away, it's.5
important to start planning early. Understand different types
of retirement accounts (such as 401(k)s or IRAs), how
compound interest can help your money grow over time, and
.how much you should be saving for a comfortable retirement
Insurance: Whether it's health, life, car, or home insurance,.6
understanding the different types of coverage available and
how to choose the right policies can protect you from
.unexpected financial setbacks
Smart Consumer Habits: Financial literacy includes.7
knowing how to be a smart consumer. This means
understanding the long-term costs of purchases, comparing
products and services before buying, and knowing when it's
worth paying more for quality versus saving money on short-
.term fixes

Practical Steps to Improve Financial Literacy

Improving your financial literacy doesn't happen overnight, but with consistent effort and a willingness to learn, you can gradually build your knowledge and confidence in managing your finances. Here are some practical steps to start improving your financial literacy:

● **Read books and articles:** There are countless resources available on personal finance topics. Reading reputable books or articles can provide valuable insights and tips on managing your money effectively.

● **Take a course or attend a workshop:** Many organizations and educational institutions offer courses or workshops on financial literacy. These can cover a wide range of topics, from budgeting and saving to investing and retirement planning.

● **Use online tools and apps:** There are many free tools and apps designed to help you manage your money, track your expenses, and improve your financial habits. Use these resources to gain a better understanding of your spending patterns and identify areas where you can improve.

● **Seek professional advice:** If you're unsure about certain financial decisions, don't hesitate to seek advice from a financial advisor. A professional can help you create a plan that's tailored to your specific needs and goals.

● **Practice what you learn:** As you gain knowledge, put it into practice. Create a budget, start tracking your spending, and set realistic financial goals. The more you apply your knowledge, the more confident you'll become in managing your finances.

The Long-Term Benefits of Financial Literacy

Financial literacy is not just about knowing how to manage money in the short term; it's about setting yourself up for long-term success. By developing a strong foundation of financial knowledge, you'll be better prepared to navigate life's financial challenges, avoid common pitfalls, and make decisions that support your overall financial well-being. Some of the long-term benefits of financial literacy include:

- **Increased financial security**: With a solid understanding of how money works, you can build a strong financial foundation that will provide security and peace of mind, no matter what life throws your way.

- **Reduced stress**: Financial uncertainty is one of the biggest sources of stress for many people. By gaining control of your finances, you'll reduce this stress and feel more confident in your ability to manage unexpected expenses or setbacks.

- **Greater financial freedom**: When you know how to manage your money wisely, you'll have more freedom to pursue your dreams, whether that means traveling, starting a business, or simply enjoying life without the constant worry of financial strain.

Conclusion: Building a Brighter Financial Future

Financial literacy is a key component of smart spending and long-term financial success. The more you learn about managing money, the better equipped you'll be to make informed decisions, avoid financial mistakes, and achieve your goals. By committing to improving your financial literacy, you're investing in a brighter, more secure future for yourself and your loved ones. Start small, stay curious, and remember that every step you take toward financial knowledge brings you closer to the financial freedom and peace of mind you deserve.

Chapter 18: Long-Term Financial Planning and Setting Future Goals

The journey toward smart spending doesn't end with mastering budgeting or avoiding impulse buys. Long-term financial planning is the final, essential piece to ensuring that your spending habits not only serve your immediate needs but also align with your future aspirations. In this chapter, we'll explore how to create a financial roadmap that supports your goals for the future, whether they involve purchasing a home, securing a comfortable retirement, or even starting a business. Financial planning is about thinking ahead and setting up the financial structures that will sustain your desired lifestyle.

Why Long-Term Financial Planning Matters

Long-term financial planning is the process of defining your life goals, setting financial objectives to reach them, and creating actionable strategies to make those objectives a reality. While it's important to focus on short-term financial health, such as managing monthly expenses or building an emergency fund, a long-term plan ensures that your financial decisions today will pay off in the future.
The benefits of long-term financial planning include:
● **Peace of mind**: Knowing that you have a financial plan in place to support major life events reduces stress and allows you to focus on other important aspects of life.
● **Financial security**: By consistently planning and saving for the future, you'll avoid financial uncertainty and build a more secure and stable life.
● **Goal achievement**: Whether your goal is to retire early, travel the world, or invest in a business, a financial plan will provide the roadmap to get there.

Flexibility: Long-term planning also helps you prepare for life's •
unexpected twists and turns. By having a financial buffer and a plan
for the future, you can adapt more easily to changes without sacrificing
your larger goals.

Key Steps to Long-Term Financial Planning

1. Define Your Financial Goals

The first step in long-term financial planning is to define what you
want to achieve. This could include saving for retirement, paying off
debt, buying a home, funding your children's education, or building a
travel fund. Be specific with your goals and set realistic timelines for
achieving them. Financial goals should be measurable, achievable, and
align with your personal values.

1. Assess Your Current Financial Situation

Before you can plan for the future, it's important to understand
where you stand today. Review your income, expenses, savings,
investments, and debts. This will give you a clear picture of your
financial health and identify any areas that need improvement.
Knowing your current situation also helps you create a realistic plan
based on your existing resources.

1. Create a Long-Term Budget

A long-term budget looks beyond month-to-month spending and
includes saving for big-ticket items and future milestones. It's
important to include allocations for retirement savings, long-term
investments, large purchases (like a car or home), and any other future
goals you may have. By having these components in your budget, you
can work toward your goals in a steady, manageable way.

Invest Wisely.1

Investing is a powerful tool for building long-term wealth. While saving is essential, investments can help your money grow over time, ensuring that you'll have more resources available when you need them. Research different investment options such as stocks, bonds, mutual funds, or real estate. Consider working with a financial advisor to help you make informed investment choices that align with your risk tolerance and goals.

Plan for Retirement.1

Retirement planning should be a key element of your long-term financial plan. The earlier you start saving for retirement, the more you'll benefit from compound interest, allowing your investments to grow exponentially over time. Make sure to contribute to retirement accounts, such as a 401(k), IRA, or pension plan, and maximize employer-matching programs if available. Estimate how much money you'll need for retirement based on your desired lifestyle, and adjust your savings plan accordingly.

Manage Debt Strategically.1

If you have long-term debts, such as student loans or a mortgage, it's important to incorporate them into your financial plan. Develop strategies to pay down debt efficiently, such as focusing on high-interest debts first while making minimum payments on lower-interest ones. By steadily reducing debt, you free up more of your income for future goals.

Build an Emergency Fund.1

While long-term planning focuses on future goals, having an emergency fund is essential for protecting your finances from unexpected setbacks. Aim to save at least three to six months' worth of living expenses in an easily accessible account. This fund will serve as a safety net in case of job loss, medical emergencies, or other unforeseen events that could disrupt your finances.

Review and Adjust Your Plan Regularly.1

Financial planning is not a one-time task—it requires regular review and adjustment. As your life changes, so will your financial priorities. Review your plan annually or after major life events (such as marriage, a new job, or the birth of a child) to ensure that your financial strategies still align with your goals. Don't be afraid to make adjustments as needed to stay on track.

Staying Committed to Your Long-Term Plan

One of the biggest challenges of long-term financial planning is staying committed. It's easy to get distracted by short-term wants or fall into old spending habits. Here are a few tips to help you stay focused on your long-term goals:

• **Visualize your future**: Regularly remind yourself why you're working toward your goals. Visualize the life you want to create, whether it's a secure retirement, owning your dream home, or traveling the world. Keeping this vision in mind can motivate you to stick to your plan.

• **Celebrate milestones**: Recognize and celebrate the small wins along the way. Whether it's paying off a credit card or reaching a savings goal, these milestones will help you stay motivated and reinforce positive financial habits.

Stay flexible: Life is unpredictable, and sometimes your financial ●
goals or circumstances may change. Be willing to adjust your plan as
needed, but always keep your long-term vision in sight.

Conclusion: Building a Life of Financial Freedom

Long-term financial planning is about more than just money—it's
about creating a life of freedom, security, and opportunity. By setting
clear goals, making informed decisions, and committing to your
financial plan, you're building the foundation for a future where you
can pursue your dreams without the stress of financial uncertainty.
Your journey toward smart spending doesn't end here. Instead, it
continues as you refine your plan, learn more about your finances, and
adapt to new opportunities and challenges. With a long-term financial
strategy in place, you can confidently move forward, knowing that
your hard work today is building the financial freedom you deserve
tomorrow.

Chapter 19: The Power of Financial Accountability

Creating smart spending habits isn't a solo journey—it often requires the support of a trusted circle to keep you on track. In this chapter, we'll dive into the importance of financial accountability and how having others involved in your financial goals can be a powerful motivator. Whether it's a spouse, friend, family member, or financial advisor, involving someone else in your financial planning can increase your chances of success and help you stay disciplined.

Why Accountability Matters in Financial Planning

Financial accountability involves sharing your financial goals and progress with someone you trust, creating a layer of responsibility that goes beyond personal commitment. This added accountability helps in the following ways:

1. **Increased Motivation**: When you share your financial goals with others, you become more motivated to stick to your plans. Knowing that someone is keeping you accountable creates a sense of responsibility and urgency.
2. **Honest Feedback**: Sometimes, we aren't the best judges of our own financial decisions. An accountability partner can provide honest feedback, helping you stay on track and making it easier to spot any spending behaviors that might derail your progress.
3. **Emotional Support**: Managing money can be stressful, especially when you're trying to build better spending habits. An accountability partner can offer emotional support during tough times, helping you stay focused on your long-

.term goals even when the short-term feels challenging
Shared Knowledge: Discussing financial goals with someone.4
else can open up new perspectives. Your partner might have
tips, advice, or knowledge about savings strategies,
investments, or debt management that you haven't
considered. This exchange of ideas can enhance your financial
.planning process

Choosing an Accountability Partner

Not everyone is suited to be your accountability partner. It's important
to choose someone who shares your commitment to smart spending,
understands your goals, and will provide support without judgment.
:Some key qualities to look for in an accountability partner include
Trustworthiness: You'll need to be open and honest about your ●
.finances, so choose someone you trust with sensitive information
Commitment: Your accountability partner should be as ●
committed to the process as you are. They need to be willing to check
.in regularly and hold you accountable
Nonjudgmental: Look for someone who will support you ●
without making you feel bad about your financial choices.
Accountability works best when it's constructive and encouraging, not
.critical or shaming
Financial Savviness: While not mandatory, it helps if your ●
partner has some basic understanding of personal finance. They don't
need to be an expert, but they should have a sense of what responsible
.financial management looks like

Setting Up an Accountability System

Once you've chosen your accountability partner, it's important to set up a system for how you'll work together. Here's how you can structure your financial accountability process:

1. **Set Clear Goals Together**: Share your financial goals and ask your partner to help you set up a system for monitoring progress. Make sure both of you agree on what success looks like.

2. **Regular Check-Ins**: Decide how often you'll meet or communicate about your progress. Weekly, biweekly, or monthly check-ins can help keep you accountable while giving you enough time to make progress between meetings.

3. **Track Progress**: Use a shared document, app, or spreadsheet to track your progress. This could include recording expenses, savings, or milestones you've hit in your financial plan. Having a visual representation of your progress can be highly motivating.

4. **Discuss Challenges**: During check-ins, openly discuss any challenges or setbacks. Your accountability partner can help you brainstorm solutions or provide the emotional support needed to push through difficult times.

5. **Celebrate Wins**: Don't forget to celebrate the small and big wins. Whether you've paid off a credit card, saved a certain amount, or simply stuck to your budget for a month, recognizing your progress is key to staying motivated.

Finding Accountability Outside of Personal Relationships

If you prefer not to involve personal relationships in your financial journey, there are other ways to build financial accountability:

Join a Financial Group: Many online and local communities •
focus on personal finance and budgeting. Joining a group can provide
a sense of shared accountability with like-minded individuals, without
.relying on close relationships

Work with a Financial Coach or Advisor: A professional •
financial coach or advisor can serve as a trusted accountability partner.
They can provide expert advice, offer structured check-ins, and help
.you set and achieve your financial goals

Use Technology: Many apps are designed to help track your •
financial habits and goals. Some even include accountability features
.that allow you to share progress with a group or community

The Long-Term Benefits of Accountability

Financial accountability isn't just about hitting short-term targets—it
has long-lasting benefits that can transform your financial future.
:Here's what you stand to gain

Consistency: Regular check-ins and the support of an •
accountability partner help establish consistent, positive financial
.habits that become second nature over time

Stronger Decision-Making: Having someone to talk to about •
your financial decisions can improve the quality of those decisions.
You'll feel more confident about the choices you're making, knowing
.that someone is keeping you on track

Deeper Commitment: The process of sharing your goals and •
tracking your progress with someone else creates a deeper level of
commitment, ensuring that you're fully invested in reaching your
.financial objectives

Conclusion: The Power of Teamwork in Financial Success

While personal discipline is essential to smart spending, financial accountability can take your progress to the next level. Whether you work with a trusted friend, a professional advisor, or a community of like-minded individuals, sharing your financial journey adds a layer of motivation, support, and responsibility that helps you achieve your goals faster and with greater confidence.

The road to financial freedom doesn't have to be traveled alone. By inviting accountability into your financial life, you're setting yourself up for long-term success, smarter decisions, and a more sustainable relationship with money. Together, you and your accountability partner can work toward a future of financial security, stability, and fulfillment.

Chapter 20: Achieving Financial Freedom through Smart Spending

Financial freedom is the ultimate goal for many people—a state where your money works for you, allowing you to live comfortably without constantly worrying about expenses or debt. But achieving financial freedom doesn't necessarily require hitting a certain income threshold or amassing wealth. Instead, it can be attained by adopting smart spending habits, making conscious financial choices, and consistently living within or below your means.

In this final chapter, we'll explore how smart spending paves the way to financial freedom, providing actionable steps to help you stay on track, maintain long-term financial health, and live the life you truly want.

What Does Financial Freedom Look Like?

Financial freedom means different things to different people. For some, it's the ability to retire early or work fewer hours while maintaining their lifestyle. For others, it's about being debt-free, having a safety net, and feeling confident in their financial future. While everyone's definition of financial freedom varies, certain core principles apply to all paths:

1. **Eliminating Debt**: Freedom from high-interest debt is one of the most important components of financial independence. By focusing on paying off loans and credit cards, you free up your income for savings, investments, and future goals.

2. **Building an Emergency Fund**: An emergency fund ensures that unexpected expenses won't throw your financial plans

into disarray. Having 3-6 months' worth of living expenses saved gives you peace of mind and protects your financial freedom.

3. **Living Below Your Means**: The less you spend compared to what you earn, the more flexibility you have in your financial life. Living below your means not only allows for greater savings but also ensures that you aren't dependent on each paycheck to maintain your lifestyle.

4. **Investing for the Future**: Whether it's through retirement savings, stocks, real estate, or other forms of investment, putting your money to work for you is key to building lasting financial freedom.

The Role of Smart Spending in Financial Freedom

Smart spending is at the heart of achieving and maintaining financial freedom. It involves making intentional, thoughtful choices about where your money goes and ensuring that your spending aligns with your long-term goals. Here's how smart spending contributes to your journey:

• **Prioritization**: When you adopt smart spending habits, you learn to prioritize what matters most. This means spending on things that bring value and joy to your life while cutting out unnecessary expenses that don't serve your goals.

• **Avoiding Lifestyle Inflation**: As your income grows, it can be tempting to upgrade your lifestyle. Smart spenders avoid lifestyle inflation by keeping their expenses consistent even as they earn more, allowing them to save and invest a larger portion of their income.

• **Financial Control**: Smart spending gives you control over your financial destiny. By tracking your spending, budgeting effectively, and reducing wasteful habits, you're able to make empowered decisions that lead to long-term stability.

Maximizing Savings: The money you save through conscious •
spending can be redirected into your savings account, investments, or
retirement fund, accelerating your path to financial freedom.

Actionable Steps for Achieving Financial Freedom

1. **Define Your Version of Financial Freedom**: Start by
identifying what financial freedom means to you. Is it being
debt-free? Owning a home outright? Retiring early? Having a
clear vision of your end goal will help you stay motivated and
focused.
2. **Create a Financial Plan**: A solid financial plan should
include goals for paying off debt, building an emergency
fund, and saving for the future. Use this plan as a roadmap to
guide your spending, saving, and investing decisions.
3. **Track Your Expenses**: Keeping track of every dollar you
spend will help you identify areas where you can cut back.
Use budgeting apps, spreadsheets, or notebooks to monitor
your expenses and stay accountable.
4. **Automate Your Savings**: Set up automatic transfers to your
savings or investment accounts. By automating this process,
you ensure that saving happens consistently without
requiring daily discipline.
5. **Invest Wisely**: Educate yourself on different types of
investments and find the ones that align with your goals and
risk tolerance. Whether it's a 401(k), IRA, or real estate,
investing allows your money to grow and work for you over
time.
6. **Avoid Unnecessary Debt**: Be mindful of taking on debt for
things that don't increase in value, like cars, expensive clothes,
or gadgets. If you must borrow, aim for low-interest loans and
pay them off as quickly as possible.

7. **Celebrate Milestones**: Financial freedom is a journey that takes time. Celebrate your progress along the way, whether it's paying off a credit card, hitting a savings milestone, or sticking to your budget for several months.

Maintaining Financial Freedom

Once you've achieved financial freedom, maintaining it is just as important as reaching it. Here are some tips to help you protect your newfound financial independence:

● **Stay Disciplined**: Even after reaching your financial goals, continue practicing smart spending habits. Avoid falling back into old patterns of unnecessary purchases or lifestyle inflation.

● **Keep Your Emergency Fund Intact**: Resist the temptation to dip into your emergency fund for non-emergencies. Having this safety net is crucial to maintaining financial freedom.

● **Continue Learning**: Personal finance is an evolving field. Stay informed about new savings strategies, investment opportunities, and budgeting tools to keep your financial plan strong.

● **Revisit Your Financial Goals**: Your financial goals may change over time. Whether you want to travel more, retire earlier than planned, or start a business, regularly revisit and adjust your financial plan to reflect your evolving aspirations.

Conclusion: Smart Spending as the Key to Lasting Freedom

Financial freedom is within reach for anyone willing to embrace smart spending habits. By focusing on living within your means, prioritizing experiences over possessions, and making intentional choices with your money, you can create a life of stability, security, and fulfillment.

The journey to financial freedom doesn't happen overnight, but every small step brings you closer to a future where your money serves you, not the other way around. Keep building on the principles outlined in this book, and you'll find yourself not only saving more but living more freely and intentionally than ever before.

Conclusion: Embracing Smart Spending for a Fulfilling Life

As we reach the conclusion of *Quit Wasting Cash: Smart Habits for Better Spending,* it's essential to reflect on the transformative journey you've undertaken throughout this book. You've explored various strategies for mindful spending, learning how to break free from the cycle of unnecessary purchases and embrace a more intentional approach to your finances.

The core principle of this book is simple yet profound: your money should enhance your life, not dictate it. By adopting the habits and practices outlined in these chapters, you empower yourself to make conscious financial choices that align with your values and aspirations. You've discovered that true wealth isn't merely about accumulating possessions; it's about investing in experiences, nurturing relationships, and creating a life that reflects your true self.

The path to financial freedom is not a destination; it's a continuous journey. As you embrace these smart spending habits, remember that consistency and mindfulness are key. It's not about being perfect; it's about making better choices over time and cultivating a mindset of abundance rather than scarcity.

Every decision you make regarding your money shapes your future. As you continue to apply the principles of conscious consumerism, minimalist living, and mindful budgeting, you'll find that each step brings you closer to a more fulfilling and financially secure life.

Ultimately, this book is an invitation to rethink your relationship with money. It's about liberating yourself from the burdens of debt,

impulsive purchases, and societal pressures, allowing you to focus on
what truly matters—your dreams, your passions, and your well-being.
Thank you for embarking on this journey with me. I hope you feel
inspired and equipped to take charge of your financial future, cultivate
smart spending habits, and live a life that resonates with authenticity
and purpose. Here's to a future filled with mindful choices, financial
freedom, and endless possibilities!